The RulEs Abide!

ThE ThinKiNg FaN's GUide to BaSebaLL RuLes
(WiTh HIsToRY, HUMoR aNd a FEW BIG WORds)

By Jim Tosches

www.TheRulEsAbide.com

In Memory of Joe & Jeannette

"Did you get any hits?"

The Rules Abide! - Table of Contents

Introduction

"[Baseball] breaks your heart. It is designed to break your heart. The game begins in the spring, when everything else begins again, and it blossoms in the summer, filling the afternoons and evenings, and then as soon as the chill rains come, it stops and leaves you to face the fall all alone. You count on it, rely on it to buffer the passage of time, to keep the memory of sunshine and high skies alive, and then just when the days are all twilight, when you need it most, it stops."

- A. Bartlett Giamatti

I've lived a baseball life in quiet obscurity. I wasn't a great player or sportswriter, scout or coach but with a little introspection in advance of my 50th birthday, I realized the game had been with me my entire life. Bart Giamatti's famous quote gets to the heart of how the game gives and takes and then leaves you high and dry when you need it most, but baseball never really goes away. Willy Loman strikes out, Apple hits another one out of the park and the Jeffersons, well, they're movin' on up in the big leagues, gettin' their turn at bat. You see, baseball is all around us, woven into the fabric that is America. In all its forms it tickles each of the senses, this baseball essence flying off in all directions and dimensions, seeping into our lore and leisure, getting under our skin; it sticks to all kinds of people and, in turn, bring all kinds back together...and that's my short argument why it has been and still is our national pastime.

My Own Private Yogi-ism

Me, I was just a regular kid who grew up in the 60s and 70s in the central Massachusetts' town of Milford and loved baseball as far back as I can remember, which is precisely September of 1967. Known as the "Summer of Love" to the rest of the country, 1967 in New England was the year of the "Impossible Dream" for the improbable run to the American League pennant by the Boston Red Sox, captured with a tie-breaking win on the last day of the season. The team featured future Hall of Famer Carl Yastrszemski, future legend Tony Conigliaro, and the big bats and personalities of Reggie Smith, George "The Boomer" Scott and Ken "The Hawk" Harrelson. Led by the Triple Crown efforts of Yaz, "The Cardiac Kids", as they were dubbed for their flair for the dramatic, captured the hearts of New Englanders, re-engaging a fan base and revitalizing a franchise. It didn't matter that the Sox lost the World Series to the St. Louis Cardinals; the course was set for the team's historic run over the next 45 years. That's right; the bastard child of the "Summer of Love" is The Red Sox Nation.

Pennant fever spread epidemically that year and even the good sisters of the Sacred Heart of Jesus School weren't immune by September's end. Baseball in those days was played primarily in the afternoons, during work and school hours, so it was a gift from heaven when the Sisters allowed us to crowd around a desk in the center of the room and listen to the World Series on a small transistor. Sister Virginia, our teacher that year, was a scary old lady to this seven year old, probably weighing in around 85 pounds in a soaking wet head-to-toe habit, old style, but feared for the shiny, steel ruler she was so expert and generous with, a southpaw I recall. Imagine Larry David as Sister Mary-Mengele from the 2012 "Three Stooges" flick, minus the "85 pound" comment, and you'll get the picture.

Virginia didn't waste her time with the skinny wood ruler from first grade but preferred the extra wide and longer metal version used in a high school math class I suppose, that hurt exponentially more than the wood one when thwacked precisely on the knuckles with short, repetitive strokes. A real pioneer, she was years ahead of the shift from wood to metal baseball bats, but I'm getting a little ahead of myself here. The only sign of her humanity was letting us listen to those games so

10

I owe her some small amount of thanks for letting the baseball rule over the iron during these welcome respites and allowing my interest in baseball to be sparked - "Thank you Sister, may I have another!"

Following the baseball-less winters that lay at the heart of Giamatti's sentiment, the first semi-warm days of spring would find lines of schoolboys, paired off in twos, playing catch across the paved yard, stretching it out for the coming season. Milford, a big small-town of about 20,000, developed a good baseball reputation in the 50s and 60s so your average dad who coached little league probably possessed a better than average baseball acumen if he was from the area. By the time I was ten or eleven I was well schooled in the finer techniques of bunting and sliding and could recite the infield fly rule in a pinch, thanks mostly to Mr. Giacomuzzi, Mark's dad. Our team, "Davoren's Pharmacy", took home the town championship in 1972 celebrated by a "we're number one", one-float parade around town in the back of Mr. Maffia's blue Ford pick-up, following his dunking in the Fino Field town pool.

Fun as they were, little league seasons ran short and hurried amidst the end of the school year so for me, organized baseball wasn't half as fun as the pick-up ball played in all its forms around the old neighborhood during the summers. These were the legendary endless sunny days of youth filled up with the simplest elements of baseball, playing catch, shagging flies, swinging the bat. If willing to bike across town, there was no shortage of real diamonds to scope out for pick-up games but humans are tribal of course so we tended to stay with our own, in our own neighborhood. The houses were packed tightly in the south end of Milford so the only fields available were those improvised; Chapin Street school-yard, too small for baseball but perfect for wiffle ball and the Rizzoli's didn't mind the fouls off their house; Fruit Street Playground, a little bigger with a green monster sized chain-link fence in right, sized right if we used a deadened street-hockey ball and wood bat; the large parking lot behind the Elks Club, ill-shaped and gravely but salvageable for batting practice with real baseballs, as long as lefties didn't pull it into the bank parking lot.

The jewel of our circuit however was about a mile down the hill from my house on South Main Street, across from Sam's Pizzeria, Vernon Grove Cemetery. Yup, dab-smack in the center of the cemetery was a good sized V-shaped lot with regularly cut grass that was undeveloped and there for the taking, in more ways than one. Right and center fields were impossibly deep but the curved access road that acted as a warning track made home run territory reachable in left for dead pull hitters like me. That lot has long since been claimed per its intended use and I would like to think that the local residents would be very happy with the idea of kids playing ball in their peaceful setting, which we loved to do back in the day when we had the luxury of a quorum, which we didn't have on most days.

Most of the time we had to adjust the game down to its lowest common denominator based on head count. Four or five could support batting practice, as long as everyone pulled the ball, three or four could yield a nice game of pickle, two was perfect for the timeless treasure of a game of catch and one, well, "one" is the loneliest number. I can't tell you what other kids did; I can only tell you how I kept up my baseball fix when pulling some me-time. To practice pitching and fielding, I found a great spot to throw a tennis ball against the back of my house from a mound of concrete about 30 feet away that served as the ramp to our neighbor's garage, which was angled just right in our tight neighborhood. The ricochet off the clapboards in such close quarters gave me goalie like reflexes on come-backers and occasionally, on a high pitch that hit just right, yielded a surprising pop-up, "I got it!" I could throw all day but my mom would put an end to it about an hour before supper because that's when she really got cookin' in the kitchen, which was at the back of the house. She couldn't escape the constant thump of those strikes but that was okay because if there was anything better than playing ball all day, it was getting the call to come in for one of Ma's home-cooked suppers, especially if she was making a gravy.

While I could wear myself out throwing those tennis balls from that mound, batting practice proved more problematic but studying the back yard environs again, I found a solution. You can't pitch to yourself of course but you can practice a swing. In order for that to be any fun you surely needed something to hit so I found a clever way to rid the yard of small pebbles - I never said I was a boy genius. The game required significant skill, naturally, because of all the houses that backed up to ours that weren't afraid to get in the way but I found a nice alley that would allow me, using my skinny yellow wiffle ball bat, to drill M&M sized pebbles all around the block in the style of my favorite Sox players. A natural righty, it was in that back yard that I learned to switch-hit, mimicking the upright stance of Yaz, the smooth balanced stroke of Fred Lynn or the hands and weight back style of Cecil Cooper (think Rod Carew), all lefties; to my knowledge, none of those guys ever put someone's eye out. The game of baseball, fully realized, demonstrates as well as anything the adage that "the whole is greater than the sum of the parts" but it was this time of my life, the golden age of my youth, that I developed my love for the game of baseball and the joy of playing it any way I could think of, rooted in the simplest component parts of the game.

Endless days of summer are mythical of course so time, she rolled on. I went on to play high school ball and a game or two in college, which you'll read about, and emerged a twenty something into a world where adults play this game called softball. Not that there aren't very competitive leagues out there or that it wasn't fun to play, it's just that playing softball always had a go-kart feel to it for me, if you know what I mean.

By the late 80s however, adult baseball leagues started popping up and in 1992 I started playing baseball again and it's been an awesome experience that has allowed me to stay active in the game into my 50s here in Southern California. I've played about a thousand games in my life and as a Red Sox fan, watched thousands more being caught up in that whole curse thing over the years. I suppose I could reminisce about the countless hours absorbing baseball at Fenway Park or about the serious and silly antics with The Brookline Tigers and Cleveland-Circle Indians in the Boston MSBL (Men's Senior Baseball League) but when you add it all up, it's simply evidence that I might qualify as an expert baseball observer under the "10,000 hour rule" Malcolm Gladwell introduced in his book "Outliers, The Story of Success." The idea that 10,000 hours of practice doing anything is the key to success is controversial but all I can say is that the more I watch baseball, the more I see; the more I see, the more I know.

Notice I called myself an observer not a fan because I'm more interested in the game itself, the action on the field, more than the people who are playing it. It doesn't matter if it's the little leagues or pros, the premise remains the same regardless of the score, the pitcher and batter will quietly stare each other down with mutual contempt masked as respect, and each will have their say. Will the hitter save the day and parade around the bases or will he whiff and have the pitcher wonder as he turns his back, "who are these buffoons who swing early at change-ups and chase sliders low and away?" In this sense, I enjoy each individual slice of baseball and the nuance contained within. This hitter-pitcher battle, for example, has been called the game-within-a-game but I like to think of it as part of baseball's dark-matter, the stuff that most of the universe is made up of that can't be seen - but we know it's there influencing everything. It is present in the quiet before the pitch, the space in between the spaces, when signs are flashing on offense and defense; with team rivalry and pitcher-hitter history hanging around like stormy weather; while the game situation, score-inning-and-outs, adds drama – the infinite possibilities of what will happen next are all coiled up and ready to spring, each pitch its own mini big-bang that spawns a new reality. After the pitch, no matter what happens, you will never have the same circumstances again so we exhale while the elements regroup and the cycle starts all over. Some people find baseball repetitive and mundane but if I may take credit for my own "Yogi-ism", I love the game of baseball because you always see something you've never seen before. You can quote me on that!

I've covered a lot of time in a short amount of space but the point is that the game of baseball has given me a lot over the years, extracted from the experience of playing it my whole life and enjoying it as a fan in the cultural environs of New England and beyond...and I woke up one day, a middle aged man, sure that I ascertained a complete understanding of the game as it is played and played-out and that I would go on enjoying baseball and all its gifts as I live out my days here in Southern California. But then something happened...my friend Michael Gervase told me about a local umpire association that works high school games and that they were always looking for new guys to train. Staring down the barrel of 50, I signed up with Pacific Baseball Umpires, literally paid my dues, went to class and field training, and became an umpire, okay, "would-be" umpire.

On the very first pitch of the very first game I ever worked, I knew I was in an entirely new realm after the ball was fouled back over the screen and for a second or two everything stood silently still while the catcher waited for a new ball. For an instant I was Leslie Nielson's Enrico Palazzo from "The Naked Gun" wondering why everyone was looking at me. "Oh, that's right, because I'm the home plate umpire." Things would get a little more serious later on during a play at the plate when the runner, trying to avoid a bat on the ground that I should have kicked out of the way, awkwardly leaped over it and into the catcher, knocking the ball out of his glove. Seeing the ball get loose, the batter-runner took a wide turn around third and was thrown out going back to the base by the alert pitcher who backed up home. "Oh dear" I thought. This was a freshman game and I was the only ump...now what? "Okay, let me think this through...by high school rule, the runner is out automatically for running into the catcher so that's interference…and since the subsequent play went against the offending team, I'll let the play stand and it's a double play albeit a weird one. Let's see, the kid who ran into the catcher didn't do it maliciously so I won't kick him out of the game. Sounds good, that's my call and I'm stickin' with it!" Like I said, it was a freshman game, the first one of the season so no big deal and no arguments from either coach.

But during the break after the third out, I started mentally parsing my high school rule book and began to doubt my first big call, which I delivered with confidence and authority. This bugged me the rest of the game like a pebble in my oversized plate shoes so after the final out, I quick-stepped it back to the car and rifled through the rule book and as it turned out, I kind of botched my first big call. When you think about it, the only reason the runner got thrown out at third was because he took a wide turn and the only reason he did that was because he saw the ball fly loose and the only reason that happened was because his teammate ran into the catcher, which in amateur baseball is interference most of the time. That whole sequence following the ball being knocked loose can't be legit if it occurred because of an illegal act, right? So, it turns out that yes, the runner trying to score was correctly called out but I should have called time out and "killed" the ball immediately and limited the batter-runner to the last base he had reached at the exact time of the interference, which very well might only have been second.

When you think this through, logically, the rule makes total sense and isn't complicated at all; the runner is out and the offense can't receive any benefit from the illegal play. How in the world would I have known that if armed only with what I learned the past forty years watching baseball? And so that is where my new journey began, not on the field, but in the parking lot at The La Jolla Country Day School, when I realized I needed to not just know the rules, but understand them…and a rules junkie was born unto us!

Umpiring has been a rewarding and enjoyable gig on a number of levels that has allowed me to keep filling in more of those spaces in between the baseball atoms, revealing more dark-matter than I had known before. Upon learning of my new venture, an old baseball buddy from Boston texted me that I had gone to the "dark side" and he was more right than he knows. That first game made me think, "I'm not playing the game, I'm not coaching the game, I'm not watching it from the stands, yet I am in the game in my own official dimension that is visible to everyone but largely unseen", which sits fine with me. All those years playing baseball and I never really noticed the umpires and I certainly never thought to read the rule book but, funny thing, they make you do that in umpire school.

As I put my new book of knowledge into practice, I was surprised by the number of little things I never really knew and when I started quizzing friends, realized I wasn't alone, "what do you mean a runner isn't always out when hit by a batted ball?" The games demonstrated over and over that the same held true with a lot of coaches, players and fans as well. The next thing I noticed was that when in doubt of the rules, fans by nature default to their rooting interest so rather than seeing the game through the prism of objectivity and proper rule, they tend to see what they want to see and rationalize a call that favors their team. Please understand I'm not trying to take the "root-root-root-for-the-home-team" out of the "take-me-out-to-the-ballgame", it's just that a better understanding of how the rules work and the logic behind them might just lead to less confusion and angst around the field, dugouts and stands, and also just make for better appreciation of the game for everyone involved. Additionally, while I always knew that little things can win baseball games, which we usually say results from hustle and quick thinking, little things can lose games too, which we usually say results from indecision and hesitation. Fogginess on the field, in whatever form, is born out of a lack of fundamentals and that surely includes knowing the rules of the game you are playing.

While there are only about a thousand major league players, it is estimated there are more than 10 million people who play baseball in America and tens of millions more who watch it, often 10 or 20 at a time at your nearest field. That's a lot of people who may or may not know the game very well watching a lot of players who may or may not play it very well and a lot of stuff happens at the amateur level that you won't see when watching your favorite team on TV. I can tell you that I look at the game in a whole new light now as I watch baseball plays develop; I see the rules as a layer of superglue that holds the game together in a way I never realized before and I thought it would be something worthwhile to deconstruct and share with you to help you better enjoy the game in whatever capacity you enjoy it. Please note that this is not a substitute for the rule book, which is a bland and intolerable read, **although I have bolded references to the rules whether taken word from word or paraphrased.**

Instead, this book explains why the rules are the way they are and the logical effect they have on the action and essence of the game. I've tried to avoid as much ticky-tack stuff as I could as that's what actual rule books are for. This is also not "Baseball for Dum-Dums" as I'm assuming you have a basic understanding about the way the game is played. In fact, I'm writing it for those who are like me, who have loved the game their whole life, know the game, and simply assumed all along they had a good understanding of the rules, but never really peaked into the dark recesses of the rule book to make sure; for those of you who are naturally drawn to baseball discussions and would especially enjoy a hearty stew containing chunks of baseball lore and history, with a little strategy sauce on the side, all peppered with personal odes to the game and insights on the fine line between the spirit vs. the letter of the rules. I'm going to give you lots of little things to think about that will start to add up as you make your way through each section. But the game has been around for about 150 years so I can't promise I'm going to be able to tell you something drastic, like there are four outs in an inning or anything crazy like that. Okay, well it turns out there is something called "the fourth out rule" so why don't we just get on with it...

The Rules Abide!

Part I – The Pitcher…

…Raised Up on a Platform

There's a moment before the start of every baseball game where the teams have yet to take the field and the diamond sits empty with a lone baseball on the ground along side the pitcher's mound. To me, it's like looking at an empty stage, centered with a microphone, just before the curtain goes up. There is muted activity and quiet anticipation of the performance to come that in baseball is quickly disturbed when the pitcher begins his measured walk from the dugout as the rest of his teammates sprint out to their supporting positions scattered around the field.

That generic ball(1), uniform and mundane, once put in motion with a variety of spins and release points, arm angles and speed, will be transformed into a repertoire of pitches of varying shapes that when evaluated collectively, build upon each other like brush strokes to a canvas and yield a completely unique picture each and every time out on the hill; and they're most certainly not all masterpieces. As he warms up, all eyes will be on the pitcher's every move to see what this cat, *this artiste*, is all about. How hard does he throw? Does it look like he has good control? What about off-speed stuff? What are we up against here?

When you think about it, baseball is unique as a team sport because it is the only major sport where the defense holds the ball. The evolved game is structured around the central role of the pitcher and this one player's ability to dismiss the entire opposing team. The Starter is out there for the duration, facing all comers for as long as he can - for as long as his manager will let him - against a carefully constructed succession of challengers, armed with clubs, who anxiously wait their turn in the spotlight to rebuff the best he has to offer.

In a very short amount of time, the batters will learn what the pitcher's physical capabilities are and beyond that point his success will depend largely on his ability to mix things up in a way that keeps the hitters unsure of what's coming next. Pitchers are typically developed because of their physical ability to throw a baseball faster than anyone else but their pitching skill is largely determined by their mental capacities. It is a thing of beauty to watch a "change up" that is taken for a third strike. In a vacuum, the slow ball is the easiest pitch to hit but mixed into a thoughtful repertoire, it's a wolf in sheep's clothing that freezes the hitter's brain, seizing up his ability to do anything but silently curse, as the pitch softly does its damage. Sure, there's no substitute for the ability to lay down the law with gas but you can beat them with brawn or you can beat them with brains so for the pitcher, creativity, intellect and individualism are required over and above their physical gifts which will inevitably decline over time…"Glory days, in the wink of a young man's eye." Young men start out strong but pitching smart is the key to longevity (2). In this regard, pitching baseball is on some level, a form of performance art. You see the game, the show, literally revolves around these performers, in the center of the diamond where God has chosen to place them, their position on the diamond numbered 1, raised up on a platform above every one else, on center stage. **In fact about 10 inches above everyone else (3) starting from a 6 inch by 24 inch pitching plate that is 60 feet 6 inches from home plate, on a mound that slopes down one inch for each foot towards the plate**. Most people don't realize the mound is not exactly in the middle of the diamond as it's a little more than **127 feet from home to 2nd**, north-south and from 1st to 3rd east-west so it's actually a longer throw to second (about 67 feet) for a pickoff attempt than it is to pitch to the batter. It's no wonder pitchers often make bad throws to second base as it's more than their 60 foot 6 inch comfort zone and during play, time doesn't permit the luxury of their habitual mound delivery when making throws from random spots in the infield. With the mound closer to home than second it also makes the throw to first for a pickoff attempt slightly backwards and about 63.5 feet, also longer than the pitch to the plate.

Sunny Days & Southpaws

Speaking of the dimensions of the diamond, let's quickly look at the layout of a field. I say north-south, east-west figuratively because in reality **it is recommended that the imaginary line from home plate to second base run east-northeast**. The best way to visualize this is to imagine a baseball field superimposed over a map of the northeast US; the line from home to second base connects New York and Boston. If Boston is second base, the first base foul line pretty much runs east-west and the third base foul line runs north-south. If you think about this, with the sun setting in the west as it tends to do, it will sink behind home plate more or less in line with the first base foul line extended to the horizon. The idea is that the field should be laid out to minimize the chance of players being blinded by the sun and this orientation prevents the pitcher and hitters from ever having to look directly at it and just as importantly protects the first baseman on throws coming across the diamond from the other infielders. Also, if you have ever wondered why lefties are called "southpaws", this is why – as they face the batter, their left arm is on their south side. Actually it's the southeast side but "eastpaw" just doesn't have the same ring to it so we'll just call it due south.

This layout does create one trouble spot however and that is right field, which in theory should see the least amount of action since most batters are right handed and more likely to pull the ball to left. Smart as it was to sacrifice right field to the baseball gods, this fewer-balls-hit-to-right theory is also the root of the time honored tradition of hiding the weak link in right field (4). This is surely a roll of the dice however; it's true, there will be fewer balls hit there but with it being the sun field and requiring the very long throw to third base, it's probably the most challenging outfield position to play, especially as the level of competition goes up.

One of the more memorable sun-field moments came late in the historic one game playoff in 1978 between the 99-win Red Sox and the 99-win Yankees; the famous Bucky-"Bleeping"-Dent (5) game played on a brilliantly sunny October afternoon before a standing-room-only crowd at Fenway Park in Boston.

The Red Sox trailed by one run in the bottom of the ninth with one out and a runner on first when Red Sox 2nd baseman Jerry Remy lined a single to right that Lou Piniella initially lost in the blinding late afternoon sun. Had the ball skipped by Piniella, Rick Burleson probably would have scored all the way from first to tie the game and the speedy Remy would have had at least a double and represented the winning run in scoring position with future Hall of Famers Jim Rice and Carl Yastrzemski due up. Piniella was quick on his feet however, in more ways than one; first he decoyed the runner by pounding his glove with his fist causing Burleson to hesitate for a moment thinking he might catch it, and then he snared the ball on one hop at the last second with outstretched arms, as if he was shouting out, "Where is it?" Had Burleson advanced to third, he would have easily scored on the subsequent long fly out by Rice but instead only advanced to third on the fly and died there when Yaz popped up to third baseman Craig Nettles to end the game. Most people remember this game for the unlikely Bucky Dent homerun but it was Piniella's play staring straight into the sun that saved the day, as dictated in the rules you could say, and allowed the Yankees to advance to the playoffs and win their second straight World Series title. The practice of constructing fields this way goes back to days when all baseball games were played in the afternoons and is still specified in the rule book today although this orientation is not as critical for some of today's modern stadiums which are such monstrosities, the high decks shade everyone from the setting sun. Certainly, older parks like Fenway and Wrigley are laid out to this exact specification but go ahead, Google-map your home town field and see if this holds true, first base foul line should run east-west, third base, north-south.

We've established the fact that the pitcher exists at the center of the baseball universe (6), this shining star, so we can now begin to talk about the rules of nature that must govern the objects that spin round him. Since the object of the game at its core is to solve the pitcher, and since the game itself starts and stops with each pitch, it is of fundamental importance to the integrity of the game that the rules of baseball establish a protocol that governs all aspects of the pitcher in this central role. It is the strict adherence to these rules that creates both the baseline for the action and scripts the pace and tempo of the game, like a metronome clicking out beats; creating, at its best, a melody or a hook, like in a pop song, that captures our attention and draws us in without us ever understanding why. In science there are laws that cannot be broken encapsulated by the statement that "water always seeks its own level." In baseball, a game that naturally favors the pitcher, the rules are set to level the playing field allowing the elements – these hitters and their batting averages - to seek their own level, in the spirit of fairness. All things being equal, the pitcher is regulated so he cannot trick or deceive the hitters and runners, despite the fact that his primary objective is... to trick and deceive the hitters and runners. So what gives?

"A" is not for Abner – The Knickerbocker Rules

I can only speculate that early baseball games were chaotic, like backyard wiffle ball games where the rules are made up as you go, double in the trees, triple off the fence; "is everyone okay that it's a dinger if it hits Mr. Murray's Buick?" I can imagine that on about the very first pitch of the very first baseball game the hurler quick-pitched the striker who was attending to his mustache in the batter's area. *"Great hornspoon! You just gazoozled me!"* And after lengthy reprieve, the second pitch ever thrown sailed by the batter's head, knocking him on his arse. *"Bejabbers! If you knock the striker with that ball, he should ripple the current over to the first square as retribution"* might have been the suggestion from the batting team's captain, marking the first time a manager begged for a favorable ruling. And then moments later, after the very first hit-batsman, the pitcher stepped towards the plate but spun and threw to the first square, picking off the gentleman who was again attending to his mustache. *"Dad-sizzle! You are a wily one and I was fooled once more by your cunning!"*... and then he briskly approached the pitcher where a polite but pithy quarrel broke out that lasted until darkness.

And so without regulations, the early baseballers would naturally do anything they could think of to gain an edge – "steal the eyeballs out of your head if they could", as my dear old dad used to say - until finally, someone took control of matters and decided it might be in the game's best interest to put some simple rules in place to create and standardize a structure that would allow the game to play out in a fair and controlled manner.

That someone was you-know-who, Alexander Cartright (1820-1892), the man officially recognized as the father of baseball. What's that you say, you thought it was Abner Doubleday (1819-1893)? Without diving too deep into the game's early history, we can indeed go back to those handlebar mustache days of 1845 to find the first formalized rule set known as the Knickerbocker Rules, championed by New York fireman and founder of the Knickerbocker Base Ball Club, Alexander Cartright.

The first formal game is reported to have been played on June 19th, 1846 in Hoboken, New Jersey where the "New York Nine" ironically trounced Cartwright's club 23-1. Yes, many historians indeed credit Cartright as the father of baseball for his efforts to diagram the field, organize clubs and games as well as to codify a set of rules. Most of us give credit to Doubleday as such, his name synonymous with baseball ever since a 1907 report, commissioned by the National League, which identified him as the founder of baseball. Doubleday however, a civil war general from the north, personally never claimed to have invented baseball and no reference to the game was ever found in any of his letters or papers discovered after his death. Over time, opinions amongst historians shifted and the tipping point came in 1953 when the United States Congress officially declared Cartright as the inventor of baseball. The Knickerbocker Rules introduced many fundamental elements of the game that have survived the last 150 plus years. Here are a few:

- The base layout and distance: 42 paces from home to second base. At 3 feet per pace, 126 feet approximates the current length and width of the diamond: 127 feet, 3 3/8th inches)
- What's fair or foul: "a ball knocked out of the field or outside the range of the first and third base is foul"
- The batting order: "players must take their strike in regular turn."
- Three strikes and you're out: "Three balls being struck at and missed, the last one caught is a hand-out"; an out in the hand, a "hand out", makes total sense I wish it had stuck.

What's amazing is this last rule specifically stated that if the third strike was not caught, "it is considered fair and the striker bound to run" which has withstood the test of time and is still true today, most of the time as you should know, but I'll cover later to remind you.

Anyway, my off-the-cuff speculation on those early days of baseball is probably not far from the truth. As the game caught on and the skill level of the participants naturally increased, the rules required fine-tuning accordingly. We can see that the pitching motion shrunk from a running start from within a long since extinct pitching box, a la cricket, to a start from the pitcher's plate with exaggerated wind-ups, to the current limitation of one small step back and one forward. As pitchers got better, the number of balls required for a walk went from nine to eight, to six, five, and finally, in 1889, to four. While the exact genealogy of baseball is subject to debate, The Knickerbocker Rules of 1845 signified that baseball had made the transition from an amalgamation of earlier folk games to that of a widely recognized and popular sport that would, as soon as 1856, be referred to as America's national pastime. The baseball rule book is a living, breathing thing, born in 1845 that continues to evolve to this day, most recently as 2013 when fakes to third were outlawed. We'll get to that one soon enough but let's begin to look at the specifics of the pitching regulations. Also, if you are interested in learning more of the early history of the game, a good source is the 2005 book "Baseball Before We Knew It: A Search for the Roots of the Game" by David Block, University of Nebraska Press (ISBN 0-8032-1339-5).

Men of Steel, Rubber & Spit

When beginning the discussion about the how the modern day rules regulate "pitching" the baseball, we need to first look at the rules that regulate the pitcher himself. His mere presence on the mound bestows upon him two personas, one as ordinary infielder, and one as the pitcher, man of steel. He "plugs in" as the pitcher by intentionally engaging the pitching plate and this is when the "pitching" regulations kick in. By the way, baseball rule books tend to use the term "the pitching plate" which is too formal a term for me so lets just call it what it is, "the rubber."

There are two implications for Ace out there on the hill when he is not on the rubber. First, he is now considered an infielder so all the rules that apply to all other fielders, which we will cover throughout the book, apply to him as well. This includes things like what constitutes a catch or who has the right of way on a play (sometimes the runner, sometimes the fielder)

28

but it also includes base awards for throwing errors which differentiate a throw from a fielder and a pitch or throw from the rubber. Not to get ahead of ourselves but if a pitcher's pickoff throw to first goes out of play, the runner is awarded one base but if the pitcher stepped off the rubber first, as lefties like to do, that same errant throw yields two bases because as soon as he disengaged, he reverted back to fielder status.

The second implication of the pitcher/fielder being off the rubber is that since he wears two hats out there, **when he has his infielder hat on, he cannot pretend to be a pitcher**. How would he do that? If he has all sorts of rules to follow when on the rubber, logic would dictate that doing anything associated with the pitching motion while off the rubber is against the rules, and it is, outlawed very specifically in the pitching regulations. The key language in the rule book are the words "on or astride the pitcher's plate"; if he straddles the rubber or is near it in any way he may not act like a pitcher, for example, look to the catcher for signs or take his normal pitching stance. In fact after a play is made and he moves to this position without the ball, as an accomplice of the hidden ball trick for example, he is in immediate violation of the rules before he does anything. This is a small example of the kind of shift in thinking I am hoping this book creates for you. Instead of asking you to remember that being on or astride the rubber is illegal as an accessory to the hidden ball trick, the principal is simply that he is out there without the ball assuming a pitching position and this is an attempt to deceive. This is easy to understand because it's just common sense and there is a lot more common sense in the rule book than you probably ever realized.

Getting back to the idea of acting like a pitcher while not on the rubber, it is unlikely you will ever see this kind of nonsense in a pro game but at the amateur level, you just might because it's a right of passage for young pitchers to try to invent some new way to fool a runner or hitter. Young as they are, they will learn soon enough that it's best not to cut class, siphon their dad's gin and replace it with water, or try any goofy antics on the mound. These tricks never work so it's best to follow the tried and true pattern of pitching that's been cooking in the rule books for 150 years.

As the rules limit any physical actions prior to the pitch that could cause confusion, they extend to his decorum as well. The pitcher is not allowed to wear anything that would be considered "distracting" and the rules specifically **point out anything on the hands, like tape and/or band-aids as well as the use of a white and/or gray baseball glove**. You might wonder why this would be the case since uniforms are often white or gray but this special emphasis protects the hitter's interests by making sure he has a clear view of the pitcher's hands. That is why **the pitcher must start from the stretch with hands separated. Since the pitcher is facing the batter in the Wind-up, it's okay to start with ball in glove.** In this same spirit, a batting glove worn underneath the fielding glove is not explicitly ruled out but is usually required to come off because it also tampers with the view of the hands. The goal is to have a clean look from the elbow down and this can get complicated with the introduction of braces and compression sleeves so popular in recent years, never mind gaudy tattoos which technically, break all the rules. Such add-ons are usually allowed so long as **the pitcher's uniform appears symmetrical**, i.e. the sleeves look the same and are approximately the same length and color on both arms and the get-up **doesn't include any exposed white or grey undershirts.** (Although a white or gray undershirt that is under a vest type uniform is okay...down to the elbow.) Got all that? As far as enforcement goes, obviously it's one thing in the pros and another in amateur ball where you are lucky if half the team is properly uniformed but it all depends on how important any given game is within the context of that league's season. Umpires usually stay away from over-officiating on these types of things and usually only demand it be cleaned up when the offensive team complains, which is usually looked at as a shot across the bow as far as the defense is concerned and that's a whole other story!

Silly as it sounds, team **logos that look like a baseball may not be used** on the front of the uniforms as that might be distracting so brilliant idea as it might be, a uniform emblazoned with baseballs would be illegal, or how about a white uniform with red baseball-like stitching going every which way? I'm not sure how much of an effect this would have in reality, it's just the rules being the rules and removing all doubt. By the way, it's not clear when the practice of home teams wearing white and visitors wearing colored jerseys originated but it could be viewed as some arcane way, from years gone by, to give the home team a slight advantage, that is if you buy into the idea that it is harder to see the white ball with the white uniform background. That theory has an urban legend feel to it so a much more viable explanation says this practice was born back when teams travelled by train and there was no guarantee the road team would have clean uniforms so gray would be more presentable after repeated wearing, if not exactly aromatic. Either way, I'll bet a scientific study would prove that the most distracting uniform to the human brain is one with a dizzying pattern of vertical lines overlaid with confusing merged letter insignia that causes nausea and random epileptic seizures – that's right, pinstripes, especially dark blue, you might say navy.

Conspiracy theories about the Yankees aside, there are a few other preliminary requirements on the part of the pitcher that you may never have heard of but are actually written in the rule book. We know it's quite common for batters to switch-hit but it is extremely rare for a pitcher to switch-pitch (7); if he can pitch with both arms, **he must indicate which hand he will pitch with and stay with it for as long as that batter is up**. Also, while we think there is no clock in baseball, **the pitcher must pitch or make a play within 12 seconds** or risk having a ball awarded to the batter as a penalty (20 seconds in high school baseball) but this applies only when there are no baserunners. **He cannot delay the game by throwing to unoccupied bases** as well and in theory must complete his pre-inning warm ups in one minute. Also, the pitcher may switch to another position and return to pitch **only one time per inning but he must, as a starter or reliever, pitch to at least one batter or until the third out has been made**.

I initially hesitated to include some of these more obscure rules that remind me of New England's archaic blue laws but then, lo and behold, as I was writing this section, one of them popped up in a major league game and was botched by a whole crew of officials. In May of 2013 in a game between the Astros and Angels, Houston manager Bo Porter summoned a relief pitcher to the bump and Angel's manager Mike Scioscia quickly countered with a pinch hitter. **The rules clearly state the pitcher must stay out there to pitch to one hitter or substitute or until the inning is over** (by pickoff for example) but the umpires then let Porter bring in a second reliever to counter Scioscia's move. After a long discussion, the umpires allowed the second pitching change despite the fact that the first reliever never threw a pitch, never mind retire a batter. Scioscia and the Angels protested the game but it was all a moot point when they came back to win the game. Hard enough to believe a major league manager wouldn't know the rules but ten times harder to explain how the umps let it slide although the crew chief was subsequently suspended for allowing it to happen. Rules like these, that govern "the pitcher", not the act of "pitching", are all in place to prevent delays and dictate pace which is so important in baseball. I mentioned earlier that the right and proper rules of baseball seek to establish a protocol for the game and these regulations address the actions of the pitcher from the time he takes his position on the field and before he has ever thrown a pitch.

And one more thing before we move on, while you probably know that the manager must remove the pitcher upon a second visit to the mound in an inning, a rule introduced in

1967, you might not know about another rule, like the last one discussed, that also requires the manager to leave the pitcher in the game until an at-bat is complete. While the manager can always go out there and pull a guy at any time, assuming he has pitched to one batter like we just discussed, once a manager makes one visit to the mound, he cannot go out there and pull the pitcher while the same guy is still up. Let's say the coach goes to the mound and tells the pitcher, "look, you're at the bottom of the order so just throw strikes" and then the pitcher immediately falls behind 2-0 and that manager concludes, "That's it! He's done", he can't go out there for a second visit to pull the guy, he must wait until that at-bat is finished. If he does goes out there, it is cause for an ejection and then the team would be required to automatically replace the pitcher after the at-bat. I think we all know about the two visit rule, but this is a twist I never knew about. And one more thing, please know the rules may be different in amateur baseball, for example, in high school baseball, visits are like timeouts in football, that is, the coach has three he can use anytime at his discretion, all in one inning if he wants, but then he has to change the pitcher on the 4th and subsequent visits.

Busted!

Now, lets move on to the heart of the pitching regulations, rules about "pitching." There are three ways to break the pitching rules in baseball, doctoring the baseball, intentionally throwing at a batter, or failing to follow proper pitching procedure. The first two are cause for an ejection, the last one is what I'm here to talk about, a balk or an illegal pitch. (An illegal pitch is a balk with no runners on which is charged as a ball added to the count but is rarely called.) I won't attempt to address throwing at a hitter. It is obviously something that plays a part in serious baseball and it is fodder for a lengthy discussion about officiating because it is all about umpire judgment and game management but the point is, **intentionally throwing at a hitter is illegal.**

Doctoring the baseball is a brazen move. That means "shameless" of course but did you know the second definition of "brazen" in Webster's is "made of brass?" This makes total sense to me now as it really takes a set of brass ones to attempt this kind of baseball high crime. Typically it can only be effective at the highest levels because the ball will not react to DNA or defect unless it's going pretty fast. I suppose it could happen at the high school or college level but it's hard to fathom amateur players having the motivation for such risk-taking given what reward? And besides, in amateur ranks, where the supply of baseballs is limited, the balls are naturally defaced after an inning or two anyways. No, this level of risk is of the plan-b or c type, when all else fails and survival carries big reward, yes, pro baseball. This would **include spitting on, scuffing or cutting the baseball, or applying some other foreign substance** that would affect the spin of the ball as it unnaturally slips from the pitcher's hand, Vaseline, Coppertone, Dapper Dan's Men's Pomade, any dab will do. I suppose it's only a baseball game and if you're gonna' cheat, you might as well go big or go home so like a three card monte pro working the city streets or a gentlemanly bank robber who works with nicely handwritten notes, there is a certain charmed respect for doing the job with a straight face in such a low-tech kind of way. We tend to be disgusted when we find out about performance enhancing drug users who have theoretically sold their souls but when we see the video of Joe Niekro busted on the mound with a manicurist's survival kit, we just have to laugh.

It seems the 70's and 80's were the golden age for these kind of outlaws and while Gaylord Perry (1962-83) comes to mind for his alleged spitball, it was Joe Niekro (1967-1988) who got caught most famously with his pants down, so-to-speak, in a game on August 3rd, 1987 while pitching for the Twins. After repeated complaints from the Angel's dugout that the career 221 game winner was scuffing up the baseball, the umpires closed in on the mound to interrogate Joe after one suspiciously jumpy pitch. Offering up his glove for inspection with an absolutely incredulous look and darting around the ensuing scrum looking for some escape from the situation, he was eventually circled by the four blue sharks and asked to empty his pockets. Down to his last all-or-nothing move, Joe turned both his back pockets inside out and extended his arms out to the side, palms up to show empty hands and in a smoothie-smooth attempt at misdirection, tossed some contraband aside. Say it ain't so Joe! If you watch the priceless video you have to admire the raw chutzpah on display because he almost got away with it, catching the attention of only one seemingly bored umpire who had removed his hat, folded his right arm under his left with his left hand up by the side of his face, Jack Benny style, as if to say, "can we please move this along and by the way, where are we going for dinner?" And then, out of the corner of his eye, he saw what turned out to be a nail file and piece of sandpaper fly out of Niekro's right hand. Joe would later admit he used the accoutrements from time to time between innings to keep his nails in prime condition for the occasional knuckle ball and oh, on top of that, because he used to sweat a lot and the sandpaper got wet, the file served as his backup. Sure it did Joe, sure it did.

You gotta love the fact that he was prepared with an alibi and was sticking with it but the league office didn't buy it so in addition to the heave-ho for that game, ultimately won by the Twins, he was suspended ten additional games that August. Niekro was forty-two at the time and at the end of a long career that spanned three decades that included two twenty-win seasons, one All-Star appearance and, what most people don't remember, a World Series ring with those 1987 champs, the Twins, something his more famous sibling Phil never did in his 318 win, twenty-four year career. Remarkable as the brothers combined major league record of 539-478 was, and is, Phil will be remembered for the knuckleball and Joe for this pants-around-the-ankles bust preserved forever on the internet.

While that was a lone incident, Hall of Famer Gaylord Perry (1962-83) on the other hand was dogged his whole career by allegations that he constantly threw spitballs. **While the rules currently prevent the pitcher from going to his mouth on the rubber (a ball is awarded to the hitter as penalty), he is allowed to do so as long as he is not on the rubber and wipes his fingers on his jersey.** It used to be that this was illegal anywhere on the mound but in an effort to speed the game up, the rule was changed a few years ago so pitchers wouldn't take long walks off and around the mound between pitches. This was legal early in Perry's career as the rule wasn't put in place until 1968 but Perry was more often accused of using Vaseline or other lubricants planted on his person, which became cause for ejection with a rule change in 1975. Perry was only caught once, very late in his 22 year career, so it's probably safe to say he got as much mileage out of the placebo effect as he did actually doctoring the ball, that is, the idea that he was cheating would have as much or more effect on the psyche of the hitters than the actual act of cheating. It was quite common to see him conspicuously running his fingers through his hair and pinching the brim of his cap with his thumb and forefingers before a pitch so whether or not he was performing Jedi mind tricks, before we even knew of such a thing, certainly, he was part of the reason the hand-to-mouth rule was introduced.

There was a time earlier in the game where it was indeed legal to throw a spitball but the rules were changed in the 1920s to make it illegal. Unbelievably, hurlers who were known to rely on the pitch were grandfathered in and allowed to continue to throw the dang thing until the last of them retired in 1934, Hall of Famer Burleigh Grimes, class of 1964. And one more interesting side note about that, once pitchers could no longer legally scuff the ball, slick baseballs became an issue so this is also the era when the pre-game practice of the umpires rubbing up the baseballs with special mud began.

Although most of the lore regarding Perry is about his creativity on the hill, one of the more interesting stories from his career has to do with him at the plate, as a batter. Perry, like most pitchers, was not a very good hitter (career .131) and legend has it that his manager in 1963, Alvin Dark, said of him "they'll put a man on the moon before he hits a home run." Unbelievably, six years later, Perry hit his first career home run on July 20th, 1969, the same day that Apollo 11 touched down on the moon with Neil Armstrong and company. True or not about the comments, if Perry was indeed supposed to be the dark lord of the mound, you'd think someone would have checked his bat for cork that day!

The Byzantine Balk Rules

Doctoring the baseball is a seemingly lost art from decades gone by and represents cheating in its purest form. Balking on the other hand is simply an example of what the military might call "FTFI", "failure to follow instructions", the rules, and is fairly common in baseball as about one balk a day is called during a typical major league season.

Balks generate great debate about what the pitcher can or cannot do while emphasis is on technicalities about the pitcher's movements, as specified in the rule books, and not about what he did with his brain, his intent. The term itself, "balk", implies an unwillingness to complete a task which on the surface in baseball is the unwillingness to make a pitch, but more specifically, unwillingness to follow proper procedure. If this is a conscious effort, it can be viewed as an obstinate act to do something deceitful and should surely be punished but if it is not a conscious effort, then it represents more of a breach of protocol which is often inconsequential to the action. This represents a philosophical problem in the amateur game because when strictly enforced, the penalty could amount to the death sentence when the infraction was not premeditated and didn't harm anyone. If the runners are moved up every time the pitcher doesn't exactly follow proper form, you might be tinkering with the DNA of the game itself by over-officiating. In the major leagues the professionally trained pitcher has four professionally trained umpires watching his every move so it's hard for any balk to go unnoticed. Pros more or less tow the line so more often than not balks coincide with a lack of concentration when the pitcher spazzes out and makes a move that is obviously a balk to anyone paying attention.

Premeditated or not, professionals must be held to the highest standard so if a brain fart by the pitcher forces in the winning run, so be it. This is not necessarily the case in amateur ball where the skill level varies greatly, the rules might only be partially understood by players and/or coaches and each and every umpire has to decide how tightly he is going to call it. These variables converge to create a perfect storm for balk controversy at the local level. I won't attempt to address all of that; I'm just here to explain the rules!

My good buddy Gene, a smart and salty, grey bearded attorney-slash-actor-slash-boat-captain, who ran the Brookline Tigers senior league team back in Boston use to gripe over post-game beers that the balk rule was "expletive-Byzantine" because it was so difficult to understand. We used to think of ourselves as "men of good cheer" when enjoying post-game refreshments but what could start off at beer-one as a scholarly roundtable discussion about the game just played could, several beers later, find Gene pounding his fist on the table and loudly calling us all a bunch of blankety-blanks after his proposed pickoff play was dubbed "preposterous" by Fred, who knew just how to push his buttons. One or two more and Gene might be quietly tutoring the younger guys about second wives and their tendency to view men as poor misshapen individuals who needed saving but by last call, typically a Grand Marnier, things may have lightened up and it might find a handful of grown men in baseball uniforms alone on the dance floor in an Irish bar…at

1:30 in the morning…on a Wednesday night…which certainly proved that we were men of good cheer in the end…but I digress.

Gene used the term Byzantine to describe the balk rule, which Webster's defines as "characterized by a devious and usually surreptitious manner." "Surreptitious" is defined as "clandestine" which in turn is defined as "conducted with secrecy." Gene saw the balk rule as a riddle wrapped in a mystery inside an enigma but what he did not understand, like lots of baseball fans, is that the idea of a balk rule is a trick question because there is no singular "balk rule" but instead a whole chapter of the rule book dedicated to pitching dos and don't that must be understood collectively and contextually to make any sense. I mentioned earlier that these regulations go back to the handlebar mustache days of 1845 and have evolved ever since, including this past year, but to see how tenuous the rules can be, we can look to 1987 when the Cardinals manager Whitey Herzog complained that the Twin's Bert Blylevin got away with 19 balks in that year's World Series by not stopping after the stretch. Hmmm, an '87 Twins pitcher accused of cheating, wait - where have I heard that before? Anyway, a change in the wording that off season, calling for the pitcher to make a "discernable" stop resulted in a record number of balks in '88, over nine hundred in the major leagues as compared to three hundred plus the year before. In many ways we think of baseball as poetry in motion - think Ted Williams' swing or that iconic Willie Mays catch - but balks are a uniquely technical fly in the ointment of our beloved game.

As much as I like to harp on about the pitcher's intent, we need to first establish a baseline of knowledge about what the pitcher can or cannot do before we attempt to pass judgment on his motivation. We all know an obvious balk when we see one, but who can say they fully understand the alleged 37 ways to balk (8)? Fun as it starts out, the 37-ways-to-balk exercise is another trick question because it's an attempt to prove a negative, what's NOT legal, so rather than straining to identify all the exceptions, what if we flipped the conversation around and have a discussion about what makes for a proper delivery? If you know how the whole pitching delivery is supposed to go down, then it's a much easier thought process to simply identify everything else, all the exceptions, as balks.

There is definite truth to the statement that if it looks funny, it's probably a balk but like all accusations in life, you better be able to back it up with something of substance in order to make your case stick. I'm always amused when half the stands are screaming out for a balk when the pitcher clearly stepped back off the rubber – fun as it is to heckle, what are they basing that on? Oh yes, the default to their rooting interest, I remember now. By dissecting the pitching regulations, we can establish a simple template that identifies each step of the delivery and makes spotting a balk as easy as 1-2-3, engage – pause – pitch or don't pitch. It's not quite that simple but a shift in your point of view will make interpreting the rules a lot simpler, going from the abstract to the linear if you will. Poor Gene! I suppose, as an attorney, he had a natural itch to master the letter of the law in order to subjugate the spirit of it, like pitchers have been trying to do for the past 150 years, but as a baseball fan his pain could have been eased by simply reading the rule book. The rules abide once again!

It's the feet stupid!

There are only two legal pitching positions, **the Wind-up**, typically used when there are no runners on, and **the Set** (aka The Stretch), typically used when a pitcher wants to keep a runner close to the base, but either may be used at any time. Before discussing these, it is critical that you understand the definition of the term **"pivot" foot** which is something that most baseball players and fans have never heard of, yet the pitching motion itself as well as the rules revolves around it. **The foot that the pitcher uses to push off the rubber is known as the "pivot" foot** because it is in contact with the

40

rubber throughout the delivery and is the foot that the pitcher *pivots* on when shifting his weight and ultimately delivering a pitch. **"Push-foot"** would have been a better name as it's the left-foot for left-handed pitchers and the right-foot for right-handed pitchers. **We'll call the non-pivot foot the "free" foot and its placement tells us what pitching position is being used.** Simple as this is, if you're not paying attention to the feet, you're not in a position to render an opinion on a suspicious move.

The key to simplifying the pitching rules is to understand that once engaged with the rubber, there are only 3 things the pitcher can do:

1. Step off the rubber
2. Attempt a pickoff or fake
3. Deliver a pitch

Okay, there are really four things he can do and that fourth thing is to commit a balk, which is any move not associated with doing the first three things legally. We already introduced the concept of the pivot foot but now we need to discuss something else that is critical to understanding the rules, the concept of **"Time of Pitch", the moment the pitcher begins his natural pitching delivery and commits him to finish the pitch**. This is the point-of-no-return that makes any attempt to do anything but pitch the baseball a balk as it is not only important to know what the pitcher can do, but when. It is also the key to determining certain base-running awards as in "where was the runner at the time-of-pitch?" which we will discuss later. Let's look at pitching from the Wind-up first since it's the simpler of the two pitching positions to evaluate.

Pitching Rules Simplified – The Wind-up

"Here's the wind-up and the pitch"…a common call when watching a baseball game and it probably triggers an image of one of your favorite pitchers in some sort of elongated pose in the middle of a delivery that is somehow unique only to them, memories from a shoebox filled with baseball cards I suppose. If pitching from the Set is designed to use an economy of motion, pitching from the Wind-up is pure free-stylin' as the rules allow wiggle room for creativity by not specifying a complete stop in the middle of the delivery, like the Set position. In fact, other than the obvious of being on the rubber and facing the batter, the pitcher can do pretty much as he pleases from the Wind-up.

My favorite pitcher growing up was Luis Tiant (1964-82), "El Tiante" or "Loo-ee" to Red Sox fans, a Cuban-born right hander who won 219 games over his 19 year career that included three 20-win seasons for the Red Sox in the 70s. "Wiggle room" indeed as Louie's delivery was downright sublime; artistic in form, genius in design as he spun and contorted to create a smokescreen of body parts out from which a baseball would appear. He seemed to have some circus-freak ability to rotate his head, torso and hips at different speeds as if they were not all attached to the same spine. Raising hands high above his head, he would turn his back completely to the hitter, bob his head with a look to the heavens and then uncoil with a leg kick worthy of a mixed martial arts KO and a side-arm, over-the-top or anything-in-between release. If you can imagine the old cartoon character The Tasmanian Devil as a pitcher then you can imagine Luis Tiant's form, like some defense mechanism evolved over eons in the jungle, designed to mesmerize and kill prey (9). Louie worked hard to make sure no two pitches ever looked the same and it was all legit as far as the rules go – truly one of a kind!

As much as I like to dissect baseball rules, there is not a lot to discuss about what might go wrong when pitching from the Wind-up, that is, until we have the pitcher in his motion and a runner on third making a break towards the plate, then we have a real "Whoa, Nelly" moment as the great Keith Jackson used to say. This is when "time of pitch" becomes critical because most balks from the Wind-up are because the pitcher started and stopped. I umpired a high school championship game in San Diego in 2012 and the only run of the game scored on a balk from the Wind-up with runners on second and third (10). The runner bluffed towards home as though a steal or squeeze-play was on and the pitcher freaked-out and stopped. This was a no-brainer for everyone in the park because he was at the top of his motion. Had this happened during any of his preliminary movements, there could be all sorts of arguments about what constitutes the start of his natural pitching motion and hence "time of pitch." Let's look at the three legal moves a pitcher can make from the Wind-up.

1. Engage/disengage the rubber

The Wind-up starts of course with **the pitcher facing the batter, pivot foot on the rubber, free foot anywhere else** (pro rule, high school and college specify the free foot must not be in front of the rubber). **There are no restrictions as to how he holds the ball** but the three methods most familiar to baseball fans are 1) both hands together holding the ball in front of his body, 2) both hands down by his side, 3) one hand in front, typically the glove hand, and one hand down at his side.

Once intentionally engaged, the only way to legally step off **is by stepping backwards with the pivot foot first before he has made any other movement that indicates the start of his motion**, again, before the time-of-pitch. **He is also expected to drop his hands once he steps off** because if you think about our pitching pre-requisites we said he cannot make any movements associated with pitching while not on the rubber. Keeping his hands together in a pitching posture violates this rule and if he were to then step back on, it might also be considered a quick pitch, pitching before taking the time to look for a sign and catching the batter off guard. Coaches take note, **the penalty for a quick pitch is adding a ball**

to the count but this is rarely called; typically the umpire simply calls time and yells "no pitch" in an effort to protect the batter, but not necessarily penalizing the pitcher. Repeated attempts would surely yield a ball call and could escalate to an ejection as it's an obvious tactic to gain an edge.

2. Attempt a pickoff or fake

This is a dirty little secret in the pro baseball rule book which allows a pitcher to attempt a pickoff move from the Wind-up position with a step towards the base. This is not legal in high school or college ball and is not something you see very often, if at all, in professional baseball but the point is that it is legal as long as it is **done before the time of pitch and he steps directly toward a base** before making the throw. The step is with the free foot of course because we know the only legal way to disengage with the pivot-foot is by stepping backwards off the rubber. Since the discussion for pickoffs is more appropriate when discussing "the set", I'll leave the details for the next section.

3. Deliver a pitch with natural pitching motion

Now that we know what the "time of pitch" is, how do we determine exactly when it is? While we can generalize and say that it is usually **any movement after the hands come together**, the rules don't specify that every pitcher has to pitch exactly the same way so it really comes down to how he normally pitches and specifically what he does before and after taking the signs from the catcher. The rule that opens the door to some ambiguity is that **the pitcher can start with his hands together in front of him or at his side.** Since **the pitcher must take his signs from the catcher while on the rubber,** a pause is created and **this is what delineates between preliminary motions and pitching delivery.** This is very important because it is this non-act, the stillness of standing and looking for a sign that is considered an important step of the pitching process. If the pitcher engages the mound with both hands at his side and then brings them up together in front of him to take signs, these movements would be considered preliminary moves and he would be allowed to legally step off the rubber. If he takes signs with his hands at his sides and then brings his hands together before starting, this would indicate the start of his pitching motion and stepping off would be considered a balk. The key to this is that he consistently uses the same motion so the players, coaches and umpires alike know what to expect. If the pitcher were to suddenly change what he does, it could be interpreted as an attempt to deceive the batter or runners and could be called a balk as the rulebook specifically reminds umpires to consider intent, pitchers and coaches take note.

That said, once the pitcher takes his signs and is engaged properly, **he can still step backwards with his pivot-foot to "step off"** or **he can step towards a base with his free foot for a "pickoff"** attempt but **any other movement begins his delivery and thus commits him to the pitch "without interruption or alteration"**, that is, his normal motion. Anything else should be called a balk.

So, going back to our "Whoa Nelly" moment, when a runner breaks from third, the pitcher can step off if he has not begun his motion or he must deliver a pitch in his usual way but with rising blood pressure at the sight of a runner taking off, there is a lot that can go wrong if the pitcher does not remain calm and composed. It's easy enough to step off, but in a rush to get the runner, **the pitcher might separate his hands before stepping off and this is a balk.** He may also **step forward with his pivot foot and this is a balk.** If he decides to pitch, he may rush his delivery, **by not pausing to take signs, and make more of a quick throw than a pitch and this might be interpreted as a balk as well.** The key for everyone in the park though is to know what constitutes the time of pitch and that the pitcher step properly.

Pitching Rules Simplified - The Set

The "Set" or "Stretch" are often used interchangeably by radio and TV broadcasters but the Stretch is actually a component of the Set, that point, typically, when the pitcher takes a step towards the plate with his free foot and leans forward to peer in for the catcher's signs. The Stretch is optional so in the rule book it's a general term that refers to **any preliminary movements before the hands have come together** and the pitcher has come to a complete stop, which the rules do specify. Let's look at the required components of the pitching motion when working from the Set.

1. **Engage the rubber with the pivot-foot**, just like in the Wind-up, only in the Set, the rules specifically require that **the free foot be entirely in front of the rubber**. Traditionally, pitchers contact the rubber by placing their pivot-foot directly in front of the rubber, parallel to it. In theory, placing the foot on the rubber perpendicular to it, like in the Wind-up is legal, as long as the free foot is in front of the rubber. High school or college rule books may specifically prohibit this. **The ball may be held in either hand but when starting from the Set, one hand must be at his side, i.e. the hands must be separated.**

2. Stretch – the position after engaging with the rubber, but before coming to the stop with hands together. This is when **the pitcher is free to make any natural movements not associated with his delivery,** like wiping off sweat, adjusting cap, motioning with either hand to wave off a sign from the catcher and most

46

importantly, turning his shoulders to check on runners.

3. The Set is when **the pitcher brings both hands together before the pitch.** The transition from Stretch to Set **must be in one "continuous and uninterrupted motion."** The pitcher **must make a "discernable stop" before pitching**. The pitcher **may not take his throwing hand off the baseball** once his hands are together, unless of course he does so to pitch or steps off.

Now, just like in the Wind-up, the pitcher can only do one of three things, step off, attempt a pickoff or fake, or deliver a pitch. When discussing the Wind-up, I said the fourth thing the pitcher could do was balk by not doing any of the first three things legally but with the Set, the list is a bit longer and includes the Stretch and coming to a set with a stop, and thus offers more opportunities to balk...if caught. There is one other specific requirement, that **if the pitcher swings his free foot behind the back edge of the rubber, he must pitch or attempt a move to 2nd.** The idea behind this restriction is sort of like what-goes-up-must-come-down, only horizontally. If the pitcher rocks all the way back behind the rubber, any attempt to uncoil towards a base, and not towards the plate, essentially adds up to a double move, and an attempt to deceive, so it is outlawed in a sense of fairness to the runners.

Also, I mentioned that in 2013 a new rule was added that addresses the old fake-to-third move on a first and third situation. This is the move where the pitcher conducts a legal fake to third and a quick spin in an attempt to catch the runner from first breaking for a steal or just a good secondary lead. Obviously this is done with the effort to trick the runner on first so it was finally outlawed and quite possibly also with the intent of speeding things up a bit as it almost never worked. **The pitcher can no longer fake a throw to third to drive a runner back under any circumstance.** Remember, once the pitcher legally disengages the rubber, he can do anything he wants; I'm talking about a pickoff move from the rubber. **As of 2013, pickoff moves to third are under the same limitations as first so now, second base is the only base a pitcher can feign a move towards.**

This new pro rule has not necessarily been adopted by every amateur league so it's quite possible, high school for example, that it's still legal to fake a pickoff move to third (check your local listings). If this is still legal, it's still a balk if the fake to third and spin to first is done in one awkward move. The fake should be one distinctive move and a turn and bluff towards first should be a separate move altogether.

Let's Count Them

Now, knowing the component moves of pitching from both the Wind-up and the Set, let's see how many ways we can find to balk:

- Before Engaging the rubber

  1. Assuming any pitching position while not on the rubber.
  2. Stands astride the rubber without the ball (remember, going to the mouth without wiping off is not a balk, but a ball will be added to the hitter's count).

- Engaging/disengaging the rubber

  3. Intentionally contact rubber with non-pivot foot.
  4. Contact the rubber without facing the batter, ridiculous as it sounds.
  5. Step off the rubber with free foot first.
  6. Change from Wind-up to Set without stepping off (sort of #7).

7. Step off the rubber with pivot-foot in any direction other than backwards.
8. Engage the rubber without the ball.
9. Drop the ball while engaged with the rubber. Also, if the ball slips out of the pitchers hand during delivery, it must cross the foul line to be considered a pitch, and most likely a ball. If it doesn't cross the foul line, it will be a balk if there are runners on base, otherwise it's a do-over, no pitch. With no one on base it would be an alert catcher to run up the line to prevent a slipped pitch from crossing the foul line.
10. Engaging the rubber with hands already together as one hand must be at side, in the Set.

- **Pickoff or fake (can happen before or after stretch so no stop is required) while engaged:**

11. Fakes a throw to first base.
12. Fakes a throw to third.
13. Makes an otherwise legal fake towards second, without stepping in the direction of the base.
14. Fakes a throw to an unoccupied base. Note, a base is not considered unoccupied if a runner is advancing toward it. A throw to third while the runner from second is breaking is legal for example. THIS IS HUGE! Read on...what I am saying here is that with runners on first and second, full count, two outs, IT IS LEGAL, when the runners break, which they will, for the pitcher to simply step towards third and throw ahead of the runner. Whether or not the umpire calls the balk is another story.
15. Fails to step directly toward the base he is throwing to. While the rule book says the pitcher must step "directly" toward the base, this is judged based on direction of the step and the size of the step. If the direction is more away from the base than towards it, it can be called a balk. (Think about a lefty's move to first, if his free foot is closer to home than first, he will be considered to have stepped towards home and thrown to first, a balk.) If the distance of the step is not noticeable, he will be considered to have not stepped at all, and it should be a balk. Key language is that the step must "noticeably gain ground" towards the base he is throwing to.

16. Fails to step "ahead" of the throw. A "snap" throw by a lefty that precedes the step, is a balk.
17. Makes a throw to the first baseman but who is playing back. If the fielder is not in a position to make a play on the runner (umpire judgment), it is a balk. If the same thing happens with either the second baseman or shortstop, it is NOT a balk. The logic is that since you don't have to throw to second, it doesn't matter if the fielder is close to the base or not.

- ## Stretch

18. Takes more than one stretch. The pitcher is allowed one stretch only. For example, if after taking the usual step towards the plate with his free foot as he leans in for the sign, he stepped back with his free foot but did not bring his hands together, that would be considered a second Stretch.
19. Failure to move to the Set position in one continued and uninterrupted move. Typical example, the pitcher is leaning in, gets the sign, starts to come up to go to the Set but decides he really wants to shake the catcher off, so he goes back down.

- ## Come to a stop with hands together

20. Fails to make a discernible stop before beginning his natural pitching motion.
21. Takes his hand off the ball.
22. Starts & Stops…Makes any movement associated with his natural pitching delivery but does not complete a pitch, either a quick start/stop or a start and then a change of direction towards a base. The pitcher is free to move his head but any movement of the shoulders would be considered a start and stop. Note, there is a new trend of pitcher wiggling the glove hand a bit once set. This is considered an adjustment and not the start of the pitch and is NOT a balk, but if you ask me, it is an attempt to deceive. Another consideration for "start and stop": if the batter steps out of the box or anyone on the offensive team yells "balk!" and causes the pitcher to stop, it shall not be a balk but an official do-over.

- Deliver a pitch

23. Swing free foot behind the back edge of the rubber and not complete a pitch or make move to second
24. Make illegal pitch with runner on base (e.g. quick pitch from Wind-up).
25. Pitch does not reach the plate or cross foul line.
26. The pitcher, while giving an intentional walk, pitches when the catcher is not in the catcher's box (lame).
27. Pitch a ball that is defaced or doctored. Note, a ball that is pitched following a balk call is considered live. That is, if the batter hits a home run, it counts. In fact, if the result of the play is that the batter-runner and all other runners advance one base, the infraction is ignored. If the result is an out, the offense has the option to take the play, which they might if it resulted in a run. Otherwise it is called a balk. This is based on the pro rules but there are variations, for instance, in high school, the play is dead as soon as a balk is called.
28. Removes pivot-foot from rubber during Wind-up. The pitcher typically adjusts his footing during the pitch and may briefly pick up his pivot foot to point it towards third, for a righty, as he re-engages the rubber; this is acceptable but if he were to intentionally remove it in an effort to plant his foot closer to home and not stay engaged with the rubber, it would be a balk.
29. Makes any move at any time that is considered by the umpire to have deceitful intent. I mentioned it earlier and it bears repeating, if it is the umpire's decision that the pitcher was doing something intended to deceive the hitter or runner, he is empowered to call a balk based solely on intent and since it will be considered umpire judgment, there is no recourse for a disillusioned manager.

When I initially set out to write about pitching regulations I envisioned a closing piece with some wily nuggets aimed at exploiting the rules to the pitcher's advantage. By diving deep into the rule book and exploring my thoughts on the game itself, I am reminded that the game is bigger than those who play it so when you play baseball well, you honor it.

My true intention is to educate and spread respect for the rules so you can better enjoy the game in whatever capacity you take it in. Sure, there are some tricks a pitcher can employ that he can probably get away with more often than not but at the end of the day, there is a difference between doing "whatever it takes" to succeed and "doing anything" to win. Rather than make suggestions about how to get away with balks, a much better proposition is to help solidify knowledge of the game and leave the technique and fine tuning to all the dedicated coaches out there. Hopefully, by deconstructing the pitching motion and shining the light of the rules on those component parts, I've helped bring the entirety of the game into better focus.

Part I Footnotes

(1) The ball is constructed of a string of yarn wound tightly around a small rubber or cork core. It weighs about 5 to 5 ¼ ounces and has a circumference of about 9 ¼ inches. It is wrapped in 2 pieces of cowhide sewed together with 108 stitches.

(2) I am reminded of Frank Tanana, a left-handed flamethrower early in his career but after arm trouble became successful as a junk-baller. This transformation coincided with personal development for Frank summarized by one of the best headlines ever, "Tanana loses fastball – finds Jesus!"

(3) Having the pitching plate raised up allows the pitcher to push off and down, using gravity, giving them more leverage and transfer of energy to throw the ball harder and with more action than if they were on a level surface. The height was lowered from 15" to 10" following the 1968 season which has been dubbed "The year of the pitcher" because the batting averages were so low. There were only 5 players who hit .300 or above but that jumped to 24 the following year with the lower mound.

(4) Also the reason why we might knock someone by saying "he's out in right field." Of course, just as you can't hide the sun, you can't hide that weak player either; at the worst possible time, the baseball gods will send the ball in that general direction and the results will surely be bad. The coach will ultimately feel punished for ever doubting that player, but have those same doubts validated as the whole team asks, "Why did you put so and so in right field?" This theory was born to me in the late innings of the 1988 summer MIT Fast-pitch Softball Championship game between the Muddy Charles Pub Red and the Muddy Charles Pub Blue where bragging rights and a big-ass trophy were at stake.

(5) Russell Earl "Bucky" Dent - a light hitting shortstop who averaged about 4 home runs per year over his 12 year career from 1973-84. Although MVP of the '78 World Series he is most famous for a 3-run homer in the famous 1978 tie-breaker v. the Red Sox. Trailing 2-0 in the 6th inning, the 9th hitter's soft fly just cleared the famous left field wall shocking

pitcher Mike Torrez and the baseball world. Making it even more unlikely, Dent fouled the previous pitch off his already injured foot and took several minutes to shake it off. Having also broken his bat, he hastily took one from Mickey Rivers, another light hitting Yankee, who was particularly hated by Sox fans for sucker punching Bill Lee in a 1976 Yankee-Red Sox brawl…hence, "Bucky-bleeping-Dent!"

(6)   Of course it's not uncommon for some pitchers to think the real universe does indeed revolve around them or that some of them indeed live in their own universe but they do have a reputation for being thinkers. I mean they called Greg Maddux "The Professor" and Bill Lee "The Spaceman" which pretty much covers the full spectrum of light that these guys emit but in the end, it's the catchers, these human rain-delays, who really try to wrestle control of the game and decision making process from the other participants. It has been said they wear the "tools of ignorance" but they get the last laugh as catchers seem to take a disproportionate amount of the manager and broadcast jobs out there

(7)   In baseball, a switch-pitcher is an ambidextrous pitcher who is able to pitch with both the right and left hand from the pitcher's mound. Four 19th-century pitchers are known to have done this: Tony Mullane in 1882 and 1893, Elton Chamberlain in 1888, Larry Corcoran in 1884, and George Wheeler. Greg A. Harris is the only major league pitcher in the modern era to pitch with both his left and his right arm. A natural righty, by 1986 he could throw well enough with his left hand that he felt capable of pitching with either hand in a game. Harris did not throw lefty in a regular-season game until September 28, 1995, the penultimate game of his career. Against the Cincinnati Reds in the ninth inning, Harris (then a member of the Montreal Expos) retired Reggie Sanders pitching right-handed, then switched to his left hand for the next two hitters, Hal Morris and Ed Taubensee, who both batted left-handed. Harris walked Morris but got Taubensee to ground out. He then went back to his right hand to retire Bret Boone to end the inning.[2] Pretty cool!

(8)   I'm not sure exactly how many alleged ways there are to balk; I chose the number 37 to honor Bill Lee who wore 37 his entire career and to honor "Cool Hand Luke" (Paul Newman), "the natural born world shaker", who was inmate

#37 in the acclaimed movie. The movie reference was actually a Bible reference to Luke 1:37, "For with God, nothing shall be impossible."

(9) Okay, not evolved from the jungle but definitely evolved...in Cleveland. After early success with the Indians beginning in '64, an arm injury caused Tiant's velocity to drop so before the '68 season he developed his new delivery, complete with hesitations, to hide the ball and mess with hitters timing. He won 21 games that year and the rest is history as they say.

(10) 2012 CIF San Diego Section Division 1 Championship game played at SDSU's "Tony Gwynn Stadium", Vista HS 1, Rancho Buena Vista, 0.

The Rules Abide!

Part II - The Batter

Just One Dying Quail!

At the heart of my brief defense of baseball as America's pastime is the notion that we love a game that advocates individualism and equality, where everyone, sooner or later, gets a chance to take their hacks. Success is never guaranteed of course but as a metaphor for American ideals and the self-made man, baseball works well enough for me. It's no small gesture that every April 15th, all major leaguers don number 42 to honor the man and the day Jackie Robinson got his historic turn at-bat. Opportunity is all we can ask for. "Give me your tired, your poor, your huddled masses..."

Baseball is a team sport of course structured around a democratic process that gives every player an equal turn in the spotlight when they step into the batter's box. Sure, volleyball rotates the serve I suppose but that player immediately disappears into the whirl of the volley where as in baseball, the focus is on the hitter and his trek around the bases. As a result there is always a little something personal at stake in each at-bat and it is the inherent struggle between pitcher and hitter that keeps me interested in any baseball game because regardless of the score, neither player is going to lie down. With all eyes on the pitch, stripped of all the ancillary distractions, the game becomes about pride and self esteem of the two primary participants. Other team sports allow players to mail it in on the fringe of the action but with no clock to milk, it's never over until it's over, so baseball demands your focused and best effort when your turn comes round. While wins and losses matter most, individual statistics convey the relative value of every player so each outcome nudges a player's reputation a little bit one way or the other.

Statistically, the game naturally favors the pitcher and baseball has been called a game of failure because the best hitters are put out seven out of ten times. Over the course of a

57

large data sampling, like say, a major league season of six or seven hundred at-bats, the difference between a player who gets two hits out of every ten at-bats and three hits is profound. .300 hitters will be millionaires but .200 hitters, well, there really aren't any because at that clip, the guy will be out of a job and/or on a bus, that is, unless he pitches, which is a different story.

The reality of course is that most players will hit somewhere in between and settle at a number that just might dodge or dip below a tipping point that seals their fate. This is beautifully dramatized in my favorite baseball movie "Bull Durham" (1988), written and directed by Ron Shelton. The story follows two minor leaguers at opposite ends of their careers: Nuke LaLoosh (Tim Robbins), the young stud pitcher blessed with the golden arm, cocky and on the fast track to the major leagues, is taken under wing by his polar opposite, Crash Davis (Kevin Costner), a wise veteran catcher who never quite made it in the bigs, brought in to mentor the kid and prep him for his future in "the show." Two points of view materialize as the story unfolds, one from a man with everything to look forward to, another from someone who can only look back and wonder "what if." Lecturing to Nuke after too much whiskey, but talking to himself as well, he explains, against the backdrop of a dingy pool hall off the beaten path, the fine line between greatness and anonymity:

> "Do you know what the difference between hittin' .250 and .300 is? It's 25 hits. 25 hits in 500 at-bats is 50 points — ok! There's 6 months in a season, that's about 25 weeks, alright? That means if you get just one extra flair a week — just one — a gork, you get a ground ball — a ground ball with eyes! - you get a dying quail...just one more dying quail a week and you're in Yankee Stadium."

The scene conveys the heartbreak of a broken dream, the fate of a man named "Crash". Fictional as the story is, the thought of being a major leaguer is a very real dream for every kid who loves to play baseball. While the balance of a pro career might be teetering on the outcome of so many at-bats over a long season in the minors, amateur baseball is parceled out in short and fleeting seasons. The games are fewer and the at-bats ever more precious, each one an opportunity to do something good for the team, impress a coach, boost one's self confidence or perhaps give the gift of parental pride to a mom or dad in the bleachers. If none of those will work, the right thing to do always is to pay it forward and extend the inning so the next guy in line can get his extra chance too. Whatever the outcome, these numbered opportunities command the batter to approach every at-bat as though it were his last because you just never know, it might be. Combined with the pitcher's equal and opposite obligations and sense of duty, we have a timeless and cardinal confrontation at the game's core.

The Nipper-Maher Incident!

One particular opportunity for me, in my youth, to do something good for the team, impress the coach, I guess you could say, all of the above, came in a college game I played in for my alma mater, Bentley College, now known as Bentley University.

This was in September of 1978 a little before the Iranian hostage crisis would doom Jimmy Carter's presidency, a more innocent slice of time when "Animal House" was a huge hit movie and lame throwback Toga parties were all the rage in college campuses everywhere. Taking Dean Wormer's advice that "fat, drunk and stupid was no way to go through life", I decided to literally give baseball the old-college-try; Bentley was Division III at the time so I figured a freshman catcher with a rag arm had as good a chance as anyone to make the team.

I had a strong arm but never a rubber one, much better suited for pitching once a week than for throwing hard every single day, especially as a catcher but that was my position in high school and I was determined to stick with it. As the first week of tryouts wore on, what had to have been tendonitis in my arm caused such severe pain that I had to stand sideways in the shower because even the slightest pressure from the water hit me like a million tiny Charlie horses punched over and over. I remember lying on my left side at night on my twin bed in my tiny dorm room as this lump of meat hanging off my shoulder throbbed me to sleep like so many sheep. None the less, I chewed aspirin like they were Pez candy and was determined to play on. I wasn't a quitter in high school as I fought back to make the baseball squad my senior year, after getting cut as a junior, usually a death sentence in high school sports, and I wasn't going to quit now because of a sore arm. Inspired by Bluto Blutarsky's rousing speech in "Animal House" - "*did America quit after the Germans bombed Pearl Harbor?*" - I thought, "No, nothing is over until we...until I...decide it's over."

My one chance to impress came with an unexpected start behind the dish in a tournament game played on a beautiful September night at Nipper-Maher Field, a fine lighted diamond on the more famous Brandeis University side of Waltham, Massachusetts. I remember being excited just to play under the lights which I had never done before so while this wasn't exactly the big time, I might as well have been trying out for the Red Sox at Fenway Park as far as I was concerned. When you have to struggle to make your high school team, you are under no more childhood illusions that you are a special baseball player. While it was an entirely different struggle to keep the pants up on the ill-fitting uniform I was hastily rationed before the game, I wore that bluish Bentley College double-knit from the 70s with pride – I was a college baseball player! Sort of.

Our opponent that night was Massachusetts Bay Community College (remember, Massachusetts is "The Bay" state) and we were ahead early on. The highlight for me is that somehow or another I was able to peg a runner attempting to steal second in the first inning, a great start and a sure omen of great things to come. It was a close play but I was thankful the call went my way as it saved me from having to make additional painful throws later on, since you don't like running into outs in baseball, especially after you've already run into one and even more so when you are behind in the game.

I think I grounded out or something my first time up because all I can remember is trying to run hard to first base with some weird gait designed to induce a wedgie and keep me from dropping trou on my way up the line. In the middle innings however we had a rally going and I came up with two outs and the bases loaded. I don't remember the count but the pitcher let one loose high and tight that tested my reflexes. As I instinctively brought my left arm up to avoid taking one in the face, the ball hit me squarely on the back of my left arm, just above the elbow on the tricep, and bounced straight down. I in turn bounced straight up and out of the batter's box towards first, very pleased with myself for the RBI. On top of my awesome assist on defense, things were really going my way.

It was the world's briefest state of splendor however. Perhaps too eager to take my base, after a stride or two, I was cut down by the plate ump who called me back to the box – convinced it was a foul ball, he ruled that the baseball bounced down off the knob end of the bat and that I was trying to steal one. I couldn't believe it but, having been coached early on to be respectful of opposing players, coaches and especially, umpires, I didn't offer much of a fight. Young as I was, I had already studied enough baseball in my life to know the umpire wasn't all of a sudden going to excuse himself, apologize for taking up my time and personally escort me to first base while massaging my arm. This is not to say I took this in stride either as I got back in the box way too fast and unfocused, that much I remember. Before I knew it, the count was three and two and I looked at a pitch I was certain was off the outside part of the plate for ball four…only to be called strike-three…loudly…for the third-out…by you-know-who. What just happened?

In an instant my perfectly good night had gone south faster than those droopy drawers I had been cinching tight all night but the fun was just beginning. My mother always told me never to feel sorry for myself because there was always someone worse off and you should be thankful it's not you. This is a heck of a way to go through life I suppose but good motherly advice none the less. As one of those naysayers always looking for a counter argument to any good and perfectly valid point, I used to reason with Ma that if her theory was played out to its logical conclusion, somewhere way, down at the end of the line, there had to be a poor soul who can't *not* feel sorry for himself because there is simply no one left who is worse off than he, the last sorry domino. In fact, whenever I would get this lecture, I could only imagine that it probably wasn't a good deal to be the second to last guy in that line of misery either, or the third or fourth for that matter. Like a neurotic "tween" channeling Woody Allen I used to think, "Sure, Ma's right but where am I in this horrific line of fate? If I'm near the back of the line, how would I know? That would suck!" As if I had anything but an idyllic childhood…

In my short and sluggish walk to the bench on the first base side of the field following my surprise strike three…following my negated HBP and RBI…in an amount of time that is less than it took you to read about my mother's good advice, I couldn't help but snap a little bit and in a very subdued outburst, employing the smallest of helmet tosses, I whined out loud …"That sucks!" Spoken quietly in my moment of grief, it was not directed at anyone in particular but in the moment-within-the-moment, was blurted out loud enough to gain the umpire's attention.

Before we go any further, it's probably a good time to introduce the Bentley coach to the story, Ace Adams, not the former Giants pitcher from the 40s but an outstanding college pitcher in his own right in the 70s and to this day, a professional pitching coach. Ace was the assistant at Bentley at the time and ran the squad during the fall. Drawing upon "Bull Durham" again, the best way I can describe Ace is that he was a perfect combo of both Nuke LaLoosh and Crash Davis. He had a golden arm and was a big time D-1 college pitcher at Michigan but was also a guy who never made it to the big leagues while absorbing a dyed-in-the-wool, old-school approach to the game. Allowing one's self to be called "Ace" is very LaLoosh-ish but his bravado was tempered with a Crash-like demand that the game be played hard, where every less than ideal effort was labeled "horse crap", which is a term somehow reserved for old-school baseball guys who usually have intimidating moustaches and like to chew tobacco (1), all this wasn't Ace's MO.

Ace was coaching third base that night so even though the inning was over, he was still well out of earshot on his way back, when things went from bad to worse. I mentioned that the umpire, whom I was not addressing at the time, heard my "That sucks!" bomb, which he naturally interpreted as "you suck and your mother sucks and all your kids and ugly little grandkids suck." As an umpire, I often accuse players and coaches of seeing what they want to see and the table was turned here as the guy heard what he obviously wanted to hear, knowing subconsciously, or consciously for that matter, that since he just blew the hit-by-pitch call, somebody would be barking at him. It's already been established that this guy's vision was suspect but so too was his hearing. Daring to compound the error of his ways and ears, exponentially at that, not only did he interpret my words as a personal attack, he wasn't even sure where it came from since I had my back to him as I walked away; he only knew it came from the direction of our bench. The guy didn't even have the good sense to assume that I was the culprit so he took a few steps toward our bench and seemingly at random, pointed out our starting shortstop, Harry, a senior, and tossed him out of the game like yesterday's news.

Enter Ace, who was just arriving on the scene from third base and wondering what the heck was going on so he took a sidebar with the umpire back over by the plate for a private explanation. I was too far away to hear the exchange but there were a lot of gestures thrown in the general direction of me and my new best friend Harry. Hands on hips, Ace turned and looked my way but I was scrambling to throw on the catcher's gear pretending to be in some stink-eye-proof bubble and also doing my best to avoid Harry who thankfully was more amused than ticked off. I sensed Ace was on his way and wasn't happy so before he could lay wrath on Harry, I quickly did the right thing and stepped in to offer an explanation as best I could. "Coach, I didn't say a word to the ump, just kind of cussed myself for taking a third strike and then I don't know, the umpire thought Harry said something to him." After a short pause, Ace shot back - "Take off the gear – you're out of the game. That's a horse crap story. You don't talk horse crap to the umpire, that's horse crap baseball." I am paraphrasing of course as that was over 30 years ago but I pretty much remember the conversation as "horse crap, horse crap, horse crap…you're on the bench…horse crap, horse crap, horse crap."

In disbelief of this sequence of events and what the coach might be thinking of me and what my teammate for the moment Harry might have thought too, I sat on that bench the rest of the night re-playing the whole scene over and over in my mind. "Oh to be the guy who *only* struck out with the bases loaded" – mother was right again, things could always be worse, and they were. I don't remember much else about that night, except that, naturally, we eventually lost the game, probably the result of an error by the back-up shortstop.

I was not scheduled to travel with the team for the coming weekend so I didn't have to be back on the practice field until Monday but by Sunday night, my arm was still in so much pain following the Thursday night game, I couldn't imagine throwing one more baseball. As a freshman living in a dorm away from home for the first time in my life, there was no shortage of challenges from handling the full college class load to working a part-time job in the school library to finding ways to get away for weekends to visit my girlfriend Deborah down at UMass-Dartmouth. Toga parties and keggers at Frank's Place aside, it was an easy decision to pass on this college baseball thing, even if it had already passed on me.

Monday afternoon I made the long walk from Spruce Hall, the most out of the way "Tree Dorm" on the upper campus, down the hill, across Beaver Street, to the athletic fields with my giant uniform under my arm, folded nice and neat. I walked out to the middle of the diamond as Ace was prepping the field before practice and arms outstretched, handed it over, like some ceremonial triangularly folded American flag presented at the funeral of my childhood baseball life...you could almost hear bagpipes playing in the distance. With straight face, I nervously spun a compelling tale of an ambitious college student who must focus on his studies at the expense of extra curricular activities as he honors his parents who work multiple jobs day and night to scrape together every extra dollar to pay for their son's private college tuition. Ace heard me out, paused for a moment, smirked and although I don't remember the exact words, said something like "horse crap, horse crap, horse crap...you're a quitter...horse crap, horse crap, horse crap."

Looking back, I guess it never occurred to me that the oversized uniform was a sign that baseball and I were not a going to be a good fit at Bentley College but trust me, there was no profound injustice or important outcome that was hanging in the balance that Thursday evening at Nipper-Maher. No other outcome would have negated the fact that my arm just wasn't in playing shape. The real moral of the story is that sometimes in life when you can't understand why things happen, much later on you can look back and see that it all fits in quite nicely. Let's take a look at the rules of baseball as the batter steps in the box for that important at-bat, because anything can happen.

The Ping of the Bat

There is nothing like the sound of a wood bat as it echoes across the ball field. Whether it's a packed Yankee Stadium or a diamond carved out of a corn field, the "crack" of the bat is unmistakable and has a natural ability to cut through any distraction; like Pavlov's dog, our heads snap towards the flight of the ball as we are conditioned to seek out the pleasure of the baseball play that will surely follow.

Equally as unmistakable is the sound of wood bat breaking as a hitter is sawed off on the hands by a fastball; like a needle screeching off the record, it's a sure sign that something has gone wrong. A few inches one way and the hitter experiences a moment of blissful numbness – feeling nothing as the ball springs off his bat – lost in the moment, he can barely remember pulling the trigger on those quick hands and getting the barrel of the bat out in front to drill a line drive to the gap or a bomb over everything. A few inches the other way and he might feel numbness as well, from the stinging in his hands as he could not adjust his swing to the location of the pitch or the speed of the ball. Stunned by the outcome he'll be oblivious to the quiet satisfaction and pride the pitcher takes knowing he has destroyed the batter's equipment. This fine line between two opposite outcomes is just another reminder of how closely contested the pitcher-hitter battle perpetually plays out.

There is another unmistakable sound in the game as well, absent from the first one hundred years of baseball, the "ping!" of a metal bat striking the ball. Originally made of aluminum, metal bats were mass marketed in the early 1970s as a less expensive (in the long run) and longer lasting alternative to wood bats, ostensibly demonstrating man's progress beyond setting foot on the moon a few years earlier and possibly one of the first "green" campaigns, seeking to recycle those discarded aluminum Christmas trees so popular in the late 60s. Equally shunned by traditionalists, the aluminum bat's economics were a hit however, so they took root and have dominated the amateur game for over 40 years.

As technology progressed and new alloys were introduced, metal bats became lighter and stronger, allowing the ball to fly faster and farther off the bat. The arms race to produce "longer" bats is not unlike the effort of the major golf club manufacturers to produce longer drivers but there is one major difference between the sports (2) and that is that there are no shortstops in golf trying to catch the ball. In baseball, you can't argue that a faster moving ball doesn't directly correlate to an increased risk of a fielder being hit by a liner so when it comes to technology here, more isn't necessarily better in my opinion. You can also make the argument that the use of metal bats dumbs the game down a bit because players don't have to develop advanced hitting techniques to be successful because the bat takes over. Instead of learning to pull the hands in to get the barrel of the bat on an inside pitch, a lazy swing can be rewarded with a bloop single over the infielder's head that wouldn't have made it out of the infield with wood. Of course, that might be the very point of using metal, more offense, but the safety issue is the greater good and, depending on how you look at it, spawned either a backlash against metal or a renaissance of the wood bat as more and more leagues choose to go back to the future with wood and more and more boutique wood bat makers pop-up like so many microbreweries.

To some degree metal bats have become a victim of their own success but even with price tags ranging north of $400, they still dominate the market in terms of numbers. The price of wood bats has also climbed with the introduction of exotic timbers like bamboo and the introduction of composite bats made mostly of wood but constructed in pieces, some even with metal handles. Like most things, you get what you pay for and while an entry level wood bat can run thirty bucks, a high end pro maple or composite bat will run well north of $100.

Traditionalists still prefer the game to be played with wood bats but it's naïve to think any debate about points of safety and performance can ignore the simple fact that a lot of money and jobs are at stake for the equipment manufacturers and their industry. I don't think you will ever see metal bats used in professional leagues but at the same time I think they are here to stay in the amateur game. Competition is a good thing as it leads to innovation and new products but until performance is standardized we'll still live in an apples and oranges world regarding the bat debate.

Science and data aside, I can tell you empirically, from my own experience, that there is absolutely no doubt the ball jumps off metal bats significantly faster than wood. I'm an averaged size guy who never hit for power but on my 40th birthday I smacked a liner about 340 feet over the left field fence in a men's league game, made possible with a metal bat of course. As nice as it felt, as did the one I hit at Doubleday Field in Cooperstown, NY the year before, you know when you hit it that you are getting a bump from the equipment. I have to admit, I enjoyed my little trot around the bases but I also knew it wasn't all me.

The next year, in 2001, the Boston men's baseball league transitioned exclusively to wood bats and the difference was obvious across the board and the games changed as a result. We saw fewer extra base hits, especially home runs, fewer liners that were too hot to handle by infielders and overall a more enjoyable game that made fundamentals and defense crucial to winning, not the ability to score runs like in slow-pitch softball. In the years that followed, I might hit an occasional double down the line but certainly no more homers.

In 2009 I went to Arizona to play in a tourney but didn't know until I arrived that we were playing in a metal bat division. Playing in a major league spring training field that was 340 feet down the line, I double over the left fielder's head in my first at-bat. In about 100 at-bats that summer using wood I hit two doubles and in one at-bat with metal, I had one double. Do the math! As small a data sample as it is, it was enough to remind me of the difference between metal and wood. Take note the next time you see a 12 year old hit a 300+ foot home run in Williamsport or a college team put up 28 runs like TCU did in a 2012 CWS game.

That said, efforts have been made in recent years to reel in performance of metal bats and render their effectiveness as close as possible to wood in a progressive step to level the playing field and make the bats less dangerous. While parents, coaches and players had to scratch their heads each spring wondering which bats were legal and illegal, beginning with the 2012 season, high school and college baseball have completely switched bat performance standards.

Beginning in 2012, the bat certification standard BBCOR (pronounced "b-b-core") has widely replaced the BESR ("beezer") method relied upon for many years. This change-up represents a fundamental shift in how performance is measured. BESR stands for Ball-Exit-Speed-Ratio, which measures *how fast* the ball comes off the bat. BBCOR stands for Ball-Bat-Coefficient-of-Restitution which measures the "springiness" of the ball and bat or the trampoline effect if you will. Without going all math and science on you, BESR was simply considered not an accurate enough measurement and yielded an annual list of exempted bats that might be different and confusing from league to league. Regarding BBCOR, think about the difference between jumping up and down on a hard wood floor and doing the same on a trampoline; the difference has to do with how energy is lost or absorbed, which is what BBCOR measures. The result of using this measure is a more balanced performance from bat-to-bat and player-to-player and a narrowing of the gap in performance from wood to metal which to some degree addresses both competitive and safety concerns. I've seen a lot of high school games since BBCOR has been in effect where both wood and metal bats were used and I still think there is a difference but the gap has narrowed significantly from where it was five or ten years ago.

According to the rules of baseball, **once a batter steps into the batter's box with an illegal bat, he shall be**

declared out if discovered. If discovered after the at-bat is completed but before the next pitch or play by the defense, like any appeal, **any positive results from his at-bat will be unwound** in addition to the out.

The only specific rules about bats typically limit the size and length. **Wood bats must be not more than 42 inches in length and must be made of one piece of round, smooth wood that is not more than 2.61 inches in diameter at the barrel** (3). While **metal bats are deemed legal by proxy with a BBCOR logo affixed by the manufacturer**, high school and college rules may specify their own diameter and length limits but of more importance is the "minus" specification that **limits the bat/weight differential at "minus 3."** For example, a 33 inch bat may not weigh less than 30 ounces so if it weighed 29 ounces it would be a "minus 4" which is illegal. Bats with ratios in excess of 3 are deemed too easy to swing, producing a faster bat speed that gives the hitter an unnatural advantage. This is the principal of the "fungo bat" traditionally used to hit grounders and flies during practice, its long length and light weight (very "minus") allow a coach to easily generate enough bat speed to hit long flies over and over. Illegal metal bats popped up from time to time during the BESR era but it is unlikely you will find any bat in excess of minus 3 with a BBCOR logo on it since it simply makes no sense for manufacturers to make illegal bats.

While rule books vary regarding mundane aspects of the bat, like how tapered the knob should be, the one most important and universal no-no is that **the bat cannot be altered from the manufacturer's original design** with one exception, the practice, originated in Japan in the 1970s, of hollowing out or **"cupping" the end of the bat**. This takes a little weight off the bat without affecting length and was legalized in 1975.

One good idea leads to another, that may or may not be good, so before there were ever accusations of "juicing" from a non-believing rival, suspicious eyes cast doubt on a hitter by suggesting "corking", the act of drilling out a core of wood from the end of the bat, replacing it with a lighter substance, like cork, and sealing and gluing the sawed-off cap back on. This essentially makes the bat artificially more "minus" as discussed above but also makes it weaker. Inevitably, a corked bat will break, so using one takes on a lot of risk for questionable reward, a gamble akin to Russian roulette because sooner or...sooner...the bat will break and the chamber will be emptied all around home plate. It's easily demonstrated that a cut ball can add movement to a pitch and that steroids can make one stronger but what do we know about replacing a few ounces of wood in a bat with what, cork or marshmallow peeps? I'm guessing that without the aid of scientific data, the few times players have been busted with illegal bats has been the result of failed experiments under game conditions just to see what would really happen as part of some double-secret-probation-lost-bet-dare in the clubhouse. I can't imagine players would be so dumb to think they could get away with such a scam over time so it's like when you see a stretch of road in front of you, seemingly clear of speed traps and you think, lets see what 110 mph feels like for a minute, this *one* time. No? Is that just me?

Anyway, bat corking has only been documented a handful of times in the last thirty years, most recently in 2003 when Sammy Sosa got busted and suspended for eight games. After shattering his bat on a ground out in a game versus the Pirates, umpire Tim McClelland noticed something funny about the split lumber. Upon review, McClelland and his crew discovered foreign materials and ejected Sosa and put the runner who scored back on third. Sosa would later explain that he accidentally used a corked practice-bat in the game and a subsequent raid of his stash of game bats came clean. Sounds believable I guess but he was also in the middle of a 2 for 15 mini-slump that included a golden sombrero plus one, a 5 strike out game, so maybe Sammy was just desperate enough give cheat a chance. Given his alleged use of performance enhancing

71

drugs as well, it's hard to tell if that big grin of Sammy's was him laughing with us or at us.

The Pine Tar Story

No discussion about the rules governing baseball bats can omit mention of the infamous George Brett "pine tar incident" at Yankee Stadium on July 24th, 1983. Not so much an accusation that Brett was cheating but a shameless and rather desperate attempt by New York Yankee manager Billy Martin to exploit a technicality in the rule book to try to win a game.

With the KC Royals trailing 4-3 in the top of the 9th and a runner on first with two down, Brett came to the plate to face the intimidating and hard throwing Goose Gossage in a classic closer-slugger confrontation between two future Hall of Famers. Moments after hitting a long shot with home run distance to left that curved foul, Brett turned on a high slider crushing one into the upper deck in right giving the Royals a 5-4 lead. As soon as Brett crossed the plate, wily Yankee manager, Billy Martin, popped out of the dugout and demanded the umpires check Brett's bat for excess pine tar.

The rules define the bat handle as the first 18 inches from the knob and specify that any tape, grip or substance, like pine tar, not extend beyond those 18 inches. It turns out that The Twins used this same tactic against the Yankees years earlier, negating a Thurman Munson hit, so it was obviously a trick Martin had been hiding up his sleeve for a while. Having spied opponents' bats and singling out Brett, the trap was set by Martin who waited for just the perfect moment to launch such a challenge. Seeing the go ahead homer fly out of the park, Martin must have choked back the canary and put on his best poker face as he approached the plate to plead his case to umpire Tim McClelland, yes, 30 years prior to the Sosa incident, the same Tim McClelland.

Home plate is 17 inches across plus a half-inch of black on both sides so it was simple enough for crew chief McClelland to measure the bat. As the umpires huddled, furor took rise in the stadium at the thought that Martin might be on to something but things really went wild when McClelland made his decision, pointed to the Royal's dugout and called Brett out, negating the homer and ending the game. The New York crowd erupted but it was nothing compared to Brett's reaction which could best be described as a conniption on steroids. Like Dr. Bruce Banner turning into The Incredible Hulk, the Bill Bixby-Lou Ferrigno Hulk by the way, the otherwise mild mannered Brett shot out of the dugout with veins bulging and arms flailing, determined to get a piece of the 6'6" McClelland. Absolutely out of his mind gone loon, it took a half dozen teammates and umpires to hold him back while arguments ensued and the Yankee faithful went wild in the stands. What was done was done for the moment. In spite of all the protest, the dust settled on an apparent Yankee victory…"The Yankees Win!"

This was not the last word on the matter however as Kansas City management was not going down without a legal fight and subsequently turned the tables on the Yankees by protesting the game. A week or so later American League president Lee MacPhail surprised the baseball world by reversing the decision and ordering the game be picked up at a later date with the Royals leading 5-4. MacPhail based his decision on the intent of the rule, which had nothing to do with a batter gaining an unfair advantage. The rule was simply in place to prevent the baseballs from being discolored and thus ruined for play or ironically, giving the pitcher a foreign substance to work with if a tarred ball stayed in the game. In light of this, while **it is still illegal for pine tar to extend beyond 18 inches** on the bat's handle, the rule was subsequently modified to specify that such illegal bats would be removed from play upon discovery but **it shall not be grounds for declaring the batter out or nullifying any action.** It's fair to say cooler heads prevailed!

The "pine-tar game" was resumed a few weeks later on August 18th back at a near-empty Yankee Stadium on a scheduled off day for both teams as 1200 people showed up for the final half inning. The Yankees went down 1-2-3 in the bottom of the 9th against Royal closer Dan Quisenberry and the game and incident went down in history, forever linking George Brett and "pine tar." There are a number of interesting side notes to the story of that game however. For one, by rule, the resumed game required both teams to use only players on the roster July 23rd , the date of the original game. Between injuries and other mid-season roster moves, The Yankee bench was decimated so Martin put pitcher Ron Guidry in center field and used first baseman Don Mattingly at second base – the last time a lefty has played second base in the bigs, a real baseball oddity. Also, Martin, still ticked off about the reversed ruling, obstinately appealed that Brett missed both first and second base, only to be called safe via the benefit of signed affidavits of the game's original umpires, who were not working the re-start. Finally, there was also the issue of the bat itself. In the near melee following the initial decision on the field and the following fit of rage by Brett, Royal's manager Dick Howser was ejected for arguing with the umpires, but also retroactively kicked out of the game was a Royal player who came off the bench amidst the chaos, wrestled the bat from Tim McClelland, and relayed it down the line to a batboy who hid it in the dugout. What kind of criminal mind would have the presence in such a circumstance to think so far ahead to hide or destroy the evidence? To interject himself into this fiasco as an accessory? It was none other than Gaylord Perry, alleged dark lord of black ops specializing in foreign substances. Gossage, Brett and Perry are all enshrined in Cooperstown but also on display, given to The Hall as a gift from Brett, is the pine tar bat itself.

In and Around the Box

So if it's not too much to ask the hitter to show up with a legal bat, let's see what he has to do to stay legal in the box. The box itself is a simple **4 foot by 6 foot rectangle that sits 6 inches off the plate and is centered on the mid-corner of the plate.** Many a coach or catcher has complained the batter is out of the box when the chalked lines are long gone so all you have to do to measure it is take one of those standard football-yard paces to measure 3 feet in each direction. Not from the front of the plate and not from the point of the plate but if you start at the corner in the middle of the plate and take one full stride towards the mound and one towards the backstop, you'll have a pretty good gauge of where the 6 foot box starts and stops.

What confuses most people about what constitutes being in or out of the box is that the rules don't say the batter has to stay in the box, but that *he cannot go outside it.* The difference between the two is that the latter statement allows for two actions that are typically misunderstood, **a foot partially out of the box and a lead-foot stepping outside the box during the swing, both legal. As long as part of the foot is still on the line, the batter is considered to be in the box.** This can look very odd when the batter sets up because in fact, since the batter's box is only six inches off the plate, it doesn't take Shaquille O'Neil batting to be both in the box and touching the plate…but this is legal. Most of the arguments about being out of the box happen after the swing of course and again, as long as part of the foot lands on the line, at time of contact, it's a legal swing. If it lands outside the line, it could still be legal if contact was made before the front foot lands. Proper technique dictates the front foot is down for the torso to rotate and the hands to come through but if a hitter's timing has been messed up by an off-speed pitch or he lunges to foul off something down and away to save the at-bat, it will surely look illegal but it might not be. More often than not, it's a bunt attempt that leads to a batter stepping out of the box because when he squares up, he turns to face the pitcher and brings his back foot closer to the plate. Instead of striding toward the pitcher with his lead foot, like on a normal swing, bunting requires the batter to step toward the pitch with his back foot...think about it. If the pitch is off the outside part of the plate, its very easy for the him to step over the line and/or on the plate to reach the pitch, especially on a squeeze play, and again, if his foot is on the ground, *entirely* out of the box, at the *time* contact is made, an alert umpire should rule the batter out. Also note that **a knee touching the ground outside the box counts as a foot**. In the bunt scenario it's possible for the hitter to drop his back knee to the ground as he squats to reach a low and/or outside pitch. Given how infrequently this actually happens combined with the fact that the plate umpire is tracking the ball into the catcher's mitt and not focused on feet and knees, you don't see it called very much. More often than not if a catcher or coach gripes about where the batter sets up in the box and he is indeed pushing the boundaries, the umpire will set him straight in an act of preventive officiating.

But that is not the end of the batter's box controversy. As unlikely as it is to see a batter called out for being out of the box, you will often see a batter swing and hit the ball and then come into contact with the ball around the plate. Most of the time, the result is a fair ball hit off the batter's foot, which is obvious to everyone. Notice I said "fair", because the batter's front foot, which is usually the one hit, is almost always in fair territory as the foul line cuts right through the middle of the batter's box. The rules **state if the batter is in the box legally and the ball hits him, it shall be called foul.**

The real trouble pops up when the batter either bunts or just nubs the ball out in front of the plate with a full swing, takes a step towards first and then touches the ball because this demands the umpire decide if the batter was in the box or out of the box. Batters will always say they were still in the box and the defense will always say he was out and the answer is usually that he was a little of both. Controversial and debated as these fair-foul calls usually are, we just covered what defines in-out of the box and this should simply be applied here as well. **If the batter stepped out of the box, and his foot is on the ground completely out of the box and the ball clearly touches him in fair territory, he should be called out.** Simple as this is on paper, half-in, half-out creates a gray area by definition so umpires will often take the easy way out and only call it when the player is completely outside the box with both feet. This might be safe but not necessarily good officiating in my opinion; either way, someone is not going to be happy with the call and a good umpire should strive to make the correct call with respect to the rule book.

While we are talking about that trouble ball kicking around the plate, also note that as the batter-runner moves out of the box and **unintentionally touches the ball while it is over foul territory, the play is dead** but if he appears to **intentionally do anything to prevent the ball from rolling fair, he shall be declared out for interference.**

Also, as he is scrambling to beat it out of the box, and his **dropped bat accidentally is touched by the ball in fair ground, it shall be deemed incidental** and the ball shall be called fair or foul not based on where it contacted the bat but simply where it stops rolling or is touched by a fielder. Note that I said "the ball is touched by the bat" and implies the bat was stationary on the ground so it is okay. However, if it is the other way around, **the ball is contacted in fair territory by a dropped bat in motion, this is considered striking the ball a second time so the play is immediately dead, the batter is out and all runners must return,** the standard "interference" call. If the contact with the bat is passive, it is deemed incidental but if active, on the throw, the batter loses the benefit of the doubt. Broken bats are a different story as you can't blame the batter for failed equipment **so if the fielder is distracted by flying bat pieces, it is all deemed incidental.** On the other hand if **the batter loses**

grip and sends a bat flying towards a fielder, the batter stands the risk of being called out for interference if it appeared to have impacted the fielder.

Are You In or Out?

There's a little game-within-the-game within the game-within-the-game, when the pitcher and batter decide it's going to be mano a mano to see who is allowed to step off the rubber or out of the box last. It's like the opposite of when two guys both insist on picking up the check and creates an awkward delay but, something has to give. As we learned in section one, the game revolves around the pitcher so he is accorded control over the pace of the game. He is allowed to step off or take long sets on top of his litany of preliminary motions so he can slow things down as much as he wants, within reason. If he goes too slow, the umpires can invoke the 12 second rule (with no runners on) and add a ball to the count. If he goes too fast, he can be balked for a quick pitch.

While it's easy to put blame on an obviously deliberate pitcher, it's the batters who largely slow games down by stepping out of the box after every pitch, to regroup mentally for the next pitch. Certainly this is within reason when it's a key moment in the game as the delay allows for tension and excitement to build in the ballpark. All the other times though, this just drags the game out and fuels the fire for those who think the game is too slow.

Personally, I don't ever remember this being a problem until two well known shortstops arrived in the major leagues, Nomar Garciaparra and Derek Jeter. Garciaparra, who had his best days with the Red Sox, was famous for his obsessive compulsive habit of loosening and tightening the Velcro straps on his batting gloves several times before each pitch. Jeter, the Yankee legend, has a much calmer presence in the box and a Zen master habit of holding his hand up, as a call for time, before each pitch. Both can be blamed for a generation of kids who take all day to get ready in the box, but the rules do not give them the same leeway as the pitcher. **In fact, batters are not allowed to step out of the box between pitches after they simply take a pitch and there is no action on the play.** You will see amateur umpires pointing to the box in an effort to return them in order to keep the game moving but technically, they must keep one foot in the box while they look to third base for signs.

While they are allowed to step out of the box, when there is some action, a foul ball, a pickoff attempt, etc, the rules don't have a specific time limit but only specify the batter is accorded "a reasonable opportunity" to take his position (pro rule, there are time limits in some amateur rule books, e.g., 20 seconds in high school.) Once he deems the delay too long, the umpire may call a strike. You can see this in an August, 2013 Youtube video you'll find by searching for "One Pitch Strike Out". In it, Oakland AA minor leaguer Vinnie Catricala objects to the umpire's strike one call, steps out of the box and refuses to return upon instruction by Blue. You could say this was another game-within-the-game, another mano a mano face-off, but there is no doubt who might win this one. The umpire rang him up for two more strikes after multiple warnings to get in the box. Cooler heads did not prevail and this led to Vinnie's ejection, but it was all within the rules.

Of course a batter is entitled to ask for time out when he needs it but will not always get it. The rules state that this is okay before the pitcher has started his Wind-up or before he has come to his Set position. This is a little confusing because it is up to "time of pitch" in the first case but before "time of pitch" in the second. The practical reality is that umpires will generally use "time of pitch" as the cut-off, that is, if the request for time is during the set, the umpire will usually grant it because the pitcher has not yet committed to the pitch. Someone will always complain that time was granted too late in these circumstances but that is usually because they couldn't hear the batter ask for time a second or two before it was granted.

If the batter assumes time will be granted and steps out of the box, it will not be a balk if the pitcher stops. If he is a high school player, he could be in for a big surprise as that rulebook declares an automatic strike if the batter leaves the box and also that a pitch delivered under the circumstance will be called a strike no matter its location. This unlikely scenario results in two strikes called on one pitch. Not pretty!

One More Thing About the Box and Interference

So while lines have been drawn, literally, to define the batter's turf, he can still find trouble and be called out for interference within his sanctuary after the pitch has crossed the plate. This usually occurs on an attempted steal and **the batter makes some movement that takes him out of his batting position and into the line between the catcher and the base the runner is advancing toward**.

Most cases of batter interference on a throw to second follow a failed hit-and-run play which requires the hitter to swing at anything to at least try to foul off the pitch since the play is designed to advance the runner by hit, hence the name of the play. If the batter lunges to reach an outside pitch, his momentum may carry him in front of the plate after he whiffs. Regardless of how he got there, **his mere presence outside the box doesn't warrant an automatic interference call** but if there is any hiccup in the catcher's release, there can only be one person to blame. If the catcher adjusts and completes a smooth release, the batter should not be called out because while out of the box, he did not interfere and obviously **if the catcher throws the guy out regardless of the batter's action, the interference is ignored.**

The throw to catch a runner attempting to steal third is more problematic because the interference can be much more subtle than when a batter steps in front of the plate. I said a moment ago that if the batter simply holds his ground he should be okay but a problem occurs when the batter tries to do what he thinks is the right thing, by taking a step backwards, but then thwarts the catcher who is also trying to do the right thing, by throwing behind the batter. It's a difficult decision in amateur baseball to take the bat out of the hands of a kid who demonstrated sportsmanship but **the rules don't specify intention and only state that if the batter's action "hinders" the catcher, it is cause for an interference call.** To abide by the rules, the batter should stay in his tracks when the runner takes off for third regardless of an old-school macho tradition that says he risks taking one in the side of the head if he doesn't duck, which is nonsense. If hitters stay put and catchers are trained to throw behind the right handed batter, all will be well!

A much more rare call is interference by the batter on a play at the plate; I've seen it happen in a few ways. The batter can somehow block the catcher out on a steal of home or one that I saw in a high school playoff game, a botched suicide squeeze, or there could be a pitch that gets away from the catcher and the batter does not clear the zone. If the runner advances to the plate and the pitcher comes in to cover and the batter finds himself in the line of a throw back by the catcher, it can very easily be called interference. What makes it worse for the offense is that there is a caveat in the rule book, specifically for the play at the plate that rules **the runner out, not the batter, with less than two outs.** Typically in baseball the offender is called out, in this case the batter, but since runs are so important in baseball, a rule violation such as interference on an attempt to score should eliminate that team's chance to score that run, so the runner is called out. **With two outs however, the inning will be over so the out is rung up on the hitter.** This goes deep into the rule book for sure but I've seen it happen and I've seen the umpires get it wrong by calling the batter out and leaving the guy in scoring position and thus giving the offense an unfair second chance to score the run with the next batter. This one makes total sense!

81

"Call 911, Our Strike Zone is Missing!"

Now that our guy at the plate is locked, loaded and ready to hit, there's an array of possibilities that can earn him first base or get him called out that have nothing to do with pitching and hitting. I'll get to those oddities in a minute but first lets talk about balls and strikes and let's call our guy at the plate, oh, I don't know…Ted.

There is an iconic image of Ted William's hit-zone on display in Cooperstown that should be imprinted upon our nation's baseball conscience forever as he is possibly the game's greatest hitter and quite possibly the last .400 hitter as well. You can find this on www.TheRulesAbide.com. All coiled-up and ready to spring, that stare alone must have been an intimidating sight to opposing pitchers knowing he could hit any pitch, anywhere in the zone. (Best bet, low or low and away with Ted.) The chart, which shows Ted's batting average based on pitch location, has a huge, old-school, strike zone that only a travel-ball parent sitting in drizzle on a Saturday morning could love, shoulders to knees. Given my earlier argument that the game favors the pitcher to begin with, obviously the definition of the zone was changed somewhere along the way in the past 50 years to give hitters a break and ensure there is enough offense to keep fans interested…I figure it must have been in the late 60s when pitching dominated. All the umpires in the stands know a good pitch when they see one but how many of you know what the rule book says about the strike zone.

The major league official rules define the zone as follows:

"The Strike Zone is that area over home plate the upper limit of which is a horizontal line at the midpoint between the top of the shoulders and the top of the uniform pants, and the lower level is a line at the hollow beneath the kneecap. The Strike Zone shall be determined from the batter's stance as the batter is prepared to swing at a pitched ball."

82

If you go back to the picture of Ted and look again at the lines drawn on his back to mark the top of his shoulders, the top of his belt and the midpoint between those two. That mid-line, right below his number 9, perfectly dissects the top ball in the zone – amazingly, the diagram accurately displays the modern strike zone as defined in the second decade of the twenty first century. With modern pitchers routinely throwing in the 90s and some approaching 100 mph, even the best hitters in the world are going to have trouble catching up to what Hall of Fame pitcher Dennis Eckersley dubbed "the high cheese", fastballs above the belt. Understandably, over time, the de facto top of the zone has come down to the belt but technically a pitch that crosses the hitter's letters while in his normal stance is a strike. In general, the strike zone starts out this big in the entry level youth leagues as rules are enforced to encourage kids to swing the bat. Batted balls and defense should determine the outcome of games, not an epidemic of walks. As the kids get older and the game is played more skillfully, the effective strike zone gets smaller.

I'll discuss how balls and strikes are called in the last section of the book on officiating but the point is, the strike zone in the rules is bigger than you think and not only that, bigger than what is even stated in the rule book. Remember, **the plate is 17 inches wide** with a half inch of black on either side making the physical plate 18 inches wide. (Technically, "the black" is not part of the plate.) Since it is only required that any part of the ball touches the zone to be a strike, pitchers are generally rewarded with a strike call when they "paint" a pitch "on the black." Given the ball is about 3 inches wide, **the effective width of the plate is about 23 or 24 inches** when you add those extra 6 inches, for a ball width on either side. Knowing from our discussion about the batter's box that its lines are **6 inches from the plate**, these lines can be used to judge inside and outside pitches, give or take an inch or three. Again, at the lowest levels where you want kids swinging the bat, anything inside the white lines can reasonably be called a strike and as the level increases, the width of the zone will decrease accordingly. There are a slew of factors that impact the umpire's judgment of balls and strikes, which I will get to, but what I'm pointing out here is that technically, the zone can be looked at as anything from just below the knees (the hollow) all the way to the letters and as wide as the plate plus another 3-6 inches. Since most fans base their idea of the strike zone on what they see when watching baseball on TV, it is easy to understand when attending amateur baseball games why there is sometimes a sizable disconnect between the umpires sitting in the stands and the one who stands right there behind the catcher..."call 911!"

The Check Swing – "Did He or Didn't He?"

The check or half swing is a tasty treat of excitement sprinkled on top of a close baseball game because it represents one of the classic gray areas of the game where both sides tend to see what they want to see. The offensive team is certain he "didn't go" and the defense will rely on some worn out line like "it would have been a double if he hit it" so the stage is set for a call that will rile up one side or the other. Arguments will be made that the barrel of the bat came across the plate or that the hitter did or didn't "break" his wrists but what really matters is **what the rules say about a swing...which is nothing.** That's right; the rule book does not define a swing.

Before we look into that, let's stop and take a step back for a second. When we picture a batter's swing we think of it in its fully realized glory, so a half swing can't be a strike any more than a broken egg by itself is an omelet. But of course the ball ended up in the catcher's mitt so obviously it was missed and the very fact that we are having this conversation means there must have been even the slightest attempt to swing so it must be a strike, n'est ce pas? Okay, I'm having fun with you because I just made conflicting statements so how are we going to solve this puzzle?

84

First, the reason a strike is called a strike is because the batter "struck" at the darn ball. Humor me here but does that make sense? When we ask if the batter swung, we are asking the wrong question with respect to the rules. The **rule book defines a strike as a ball that was "struck at and missed"** so the real question that needs to be answered is "did the batter strike at the ball?" That by itself doesn't get us out of the woods so let's look at the language. You will often hear play-by-play announcers use the phrase "did he offer" which I think is a better way to put it. Did the batter offer at the pitch? Because we know it was missed! It might appear I am leading us down the path of my earlier pitcher-friendly interpretation but I am simply trying to shift the thinking away from the evaluation of a physical act, the swing, and more towards the evaluation of the batter's intent, to strike at, and this is where the tables tip to "less is more" in my mind. A half swing does not equal a full swing but a half attempt equals a full attempt or let me put it another way, it's very easy to conclude that if you're breakin' eggs, you're makin' breakfast!

I hope you follow my thought process here but in the end it doesn't matter what I think because all it says in the rule book is that it is **umpire judgment of whether or not the batter struck at the pitch.** In the end, he is free to go to either extreme I mentioned earlier and any player or manager is not allowed to argue it because **it is a judgment call, which you can't argue in baseball.** By the way, Red Sox slugger Jim Rice's swing was so powerful, he once snapped the bat in two just by checking his swing. The old argument that "it would have been a double" if he made contact could never be more true so it's hard to say he didn't strike at the ball. I don't recall if that swing was appealed but with his surly reputation at the time and an ability to snap a neck as easily as a bat, I'm guessing an emphatic "no he didn't" would have been the call.

Okay, so I am a stickler when it comes to intent but let's go back to the physical side of the argument and look at some practical matters for how you can decide what makes an attempt and a strike. Since no two batters are alike, the one constant and fixed piece of the puzzle is the plate itself. Most of the time, the bat makes contact with the ball in the space above the plate so, if it appears the bat made it into the strike zone – forget about the ball - it's fair enough to call it a strike. If the plate guy throws the call to one of his partners there are a couple of considerations that are problematic. If behind first base, the umpire may be as far as 110 feet away; in this position he has a decent angle to see if the bat was extended into the zone and/or past the body but the game of inches is blurred when observing from so far away. If the base guy is behind the pitcher lined up with either the first or third base edge of the mound, he is closer but his angle is now too sharp and he will probably only be able to ring up obvious strikes and if that's the case, then his help won't be needed much.

It's also important to note that there was a time in baseball when umpires didn't like to admit they got anything wrong so it might have been taboo for one umpire to override another's call on appeal. With so much emphasis today on officials working together to get a call correct there can still be extenuating circumstances that cause one official to be reluctant to overrule another; perhaps the plate guy is getting the business on his balls and strikes and his partner simply doesn't want to give either team more reason to question his judgment. The officials want to get the call right but they also don't want to throw their partner under the bus either because at the end of the day, their partners are the only friends they have out there on the diamond.

"Did He or Didn't He?" – The Bunt

There is another flavor of "did he or didn't he" that is just as controversial as the garden variety check swing and that is the question of a bunt attempt.

The rule book only defines a bunt as an effort to "slowly tap" the ball so it **provides no guidelines for what** constitutes a **"swing"** so we're back to the "struck at" test. Proper bunting technique calls for the batter to square himself off, facing the pitcher, hold the bat horizontal to the ground, and "catch" the ball with the bat. Players will take these steps to line up a bunt but in an effort to affect the direction of the ball, they will punch the bat slightly forward to propel the ball up the first or third base lines. This "punch", a slight movement forward with the bat, is considered the strike at the ball and will trigger the umpire's call, usually with a loud "yes he did!" Simply holding the bat over the plate in the ready position does not constitute a swing on a bunt attempt.

Many coaches will argue that if the player did not draw the bat back and away from the pitch it should be called a strike but they have turned the rules of our society and pastime on its head to suit their own desires. The player is presumed innocent until proven guilty, triggered by the "punch", not guilty until proven innocent, indicated by the withdrawing of the bat. Of course the defensive coach wants a strike to be called, but you can't call it a strike if it wasn't struck at!

Since we're talking about bunts, it's worth reminding you that **a batter is out when he fouls off a bunt with two strikes**. The fundamental object of batting is to hit the ball as hard and far as you can. Since bunting is the exact opposite of this, the rules remove the protection of the third-strike foul in another effort to limit any benefit from not doing what you are supposed to do. In fact, this goes one step further on a bunt and is something most baseball fans do not know, **a bunt cannot result in the declaration of the infield fly rule**. The purpose of the IFR is to protect the runners when they are at a disadvantage, but since the bunt is not a bona-fide attempt to hit the ball, the offense loses the benefit of the doubt the rule accords. You might say bunts are a "cute" ploy on offense. If poorly executed, the defense is, by all means, welcome to turn it on its head by letting it drop untouched as a prelude to a double play. Touche!

Hit By Pitch – Fight or Flight!

The standard whine echoing from the bleachers when a batter is hit by a pitch is that he must make an effort to get out of the way and lo and behold this is technically correct according to the rules. The pro rule book says he is entitled to first base if **a pitch touches the batter or his clothing, unless he makes no effort to avoid being hit.** Other leagues, high school for example, use different language like he "may not permit himself" to be hit which makes a big difference when interpreting the rules literally as it shifts the basis for the ruling from the batter's physical response to his intent. As you know from watching the game, the wording doesn't seem to matter because batters who don't budge before the plunking are awarded first base the vast majority of the time, the 99.9% kind of majority.

First things first, if a batter intentionally moves into the ball, he indeed should be kept in the box and have a ball called unless he is so bold or dumb to crouch over the plate and be hit by a pitch that is in the strike zone. **The ball is always "dead" when it strikes the batter** (and all runners return to the base they held at the time of pitch) but a strike is a strike so if the pitch is over the plate or the **batter swings at a pitch that hits him, it shall be called a strike**. A pitch that hits the batter's hands is sometimes controversial and the outcome should be determined by whether he swung or not. The old debate about the hands being part of the bat is a moot point; the hands are part of the batter and if they are hit, he is awarded first base but if hit in the act of swinging, then it is a strike. The real tricky situation is where the ball gets a piece of the hands and bat at the same time. The batter will have a natural reaction to being hit on the hands, which is painful, but everybody might hear the sound of a foul ball. Impossible to tell what happened first, the batter usually gets the benefit of the doubt and is awarded first base if he wasn't deemed to have struck at the ball.

But what of the hitter who hasn't budged and got plunked? It might be a simple question, "did he attempt to get out of the way" but the real question is, "how would you know?" The reality of the situation is that a batter has less than a second to react to a pitch thrown from the mound, 60 feet 6 inches away. In fact less than a 1/2 second for a major league fast ball and less than six tenths of a second for a 70 mph pitch which might be the average fastball in a men's league game.

Because of the shorter plate to mound distances in youth leagues, the time required to react to a pitch can be even less than that required on the big-boy diamond. A half a second is not a lot of time but hitters obviously have the ability to pull the trigger on a swing on such short notice so why shouldn't they be able to get out of the way equally as fast? Well professor, simple answer: the human body is not designed to perform equally going both forwards and backwards. If it was, every joint would flex both ways and we would have been born with eyes in the back of our heads.

When humans practice anything over and over, like hitting a baseball, the goal is to develop muscle memory and quick reflexes...these only go one way as the body is not developed symmetrically; that's why we pull hamstrings, because the muscles that propel the leg, the quads, are stronger than those that pull the leg back and the imbalance in power causes the machine to break. Add into the mix the fact that as a batter prepares to swing, he is coiling up his energy so you have a trap that is set to spring only in one direction, never mind the fact that psychologically he has been visualizing a swing and concentrating on assaulting the ball with his weapon.

The very idea of recoiling is counterproductive but, as the human body is an amazing thing, we have some ancient safety systems in place in our non-conscious brain that seeks to protect us while active in our conscious humanly pursuits. This is the part of the brain that triggers lightning quick reflexes, like hitting the deck when a baseball is coming at your head or hitting the brakes the instant someone cuts you off on the highway. These reflex responses are not the result of active decision making but your brain's auto pilot taking over control, motivated by self-preservation. So, there are two options hardwired for the hitter, consciously spring the trap or subconsciously get out of the way - think about it, fight or flight.

The third option, the one everybody is whining about when a batter is hit, is the conscious decision to intentionally be hit by the ball, which is the least natural choice for any species. For this to be true, you must believe that the player, in about a half a second, had the time to recognize a pitch that was coming at him, evaluate the pros and cons of letting it hit him and then hit all the buttons that override the fight or flight responses and physically do the reverse of what he is programmed and designed to do, in a half a second? It's not unlike backing your car up, you have to first stop the car, go through a neutral phase, then engage a different set of gears which naturally are not able to make the car go as fast backwards as forwards. The batter who can accomplish this has to be one Wile E. Coyote and we're talking about guys who often can't remember how many outs there are or recognize a bunt sign, never mind think this quickly.

The batter naturally deserves the benefit of the doubt so the only way an official can, beyond a doubt, read this plunk as intentional is if there was excessive time by baseball standards, like on a floating change up or a really slow and sloppy curve ball and the batter's actions demonstrated he clearly permitted himself to be hit.

All that said, I haven't even mentioned the obvious, that the pitcher most likely not only didn't throw a strike but threw a particularly bad pitch that sailed into the batter's box. Calling for the hitter to stay in the box when the pitcher failed at his primary responsibility is essentially asking for an act of amnesty so fans begging for this call don't realize how doubly partisan they appear. This is one of those cases where the baseball rule book says one thing but the governing law is simply common sense which will serve justice the vast majority of the time.

That doesn't mean there aren't players who do try to get hit on occasion and you will see it called every now and then, but it usually requires some extenuating circumstance that plants suspicion in the umpire's mind up front. In the amateur game it might be because a particular player indeed has a history of hanging over the plate; after getting the benefit of the doubt a few times, he will be held back once this devious pattern has blossomed for all to see.

It is an extremely rare call in the big leagues. The most famous case goes back to 1968 amidst Don Drysdale's record setting scoreless inning streak for the Dodgers. In a game against the Giants, Drysdale hit Dick Dietz with the bases loaded which would have forced in a run, ending the scoreless streak at 44 innings. Knowing the situation and what was at stake, it wasn't a stretch to believe a player would do anything to get on base and break up the streak so umpire Harry Wendlestadt read ill intent into the fact that Dietz didn't make an effort to get out of the way and kept him in the box. Dietz subsequently flied out and Drysdale was able to run his streak up another 14 innings to 58 2/3rds, which stood for 20 more years until fellow Dodger Orel Hershiser broke the record in '88, which still stands today at 59. The key to both of these examples is that it took a pre-existing suspicion by the umpire in order to flip the benefit of the doubt from the hitter to the pitcher.

One other tidbit about the hit batter is that the rules seek to award the batter ostensibly as payback for the price he had to pay by physically being hit and also to penalize the pitcher and defensive team. It has always bothered me that the batter is awarded first base for a pitch that simply brushes the uniform. For one thing, this doesn't satisfy, for me anyway, the idea that the batter was hit by an ill-located pitch, only that his uniform was grazed...by a pitch often not far off the plate. There actually was a time when being hit on the hands or arms did not count as a hit batter, which is a little too forgiving, but the rule was changed around the turn of the century to what it is today.

Anyway, the close calls that graze the uniform come with big reward in a tight game and are usually only detected by the sound the ball makes as it whooshes by the batter. In my opinion, the precedent set by the foul-tip should be expanded upon and this would be a good place to start. If I were king for a day I would propose a rule change that keeps pitches that graze the uniform, and are caught by the catcher, a la the foul tip, in play and not grounds for awarding first base. Call me a rebel but if truly plunked, the ball will not be catchable. In my opinion, this would simplify officiating and add a few grams of fairness to the scales of baseball justice that currently dish out the full award of a free pass for a hit-by-pitch that seemingly qualifies only on a technicality. I have a similar radical proposal coming up in the section on dropped third strikes.

Before we leave the topic of hit batters I want to bring up a modern concern that doesn't seem to be addressed specifically in the rules, beards and hair. I've seen lots of guys these days with long hair pulled back into a ponytail that hangs down their back and beards that hang off the chin pharaoh style and have always wondered what I would do if a pitch clips one of these. My first instinct tells me that it's no different than the uniform that gets nipped and you know where I stand on that, but as the rule is written, "hits the batter or his clothing", implies it is part of the batter's person so I believe he should be sent to first base. This is how it works by the way in women's fast pitch softball where there is a preponderance of ponytails.

Infield Fly Rule & The Infield Strike Rule

I said in my introduction that this book was no attempt at "Baseball for Dum-Dums" so we shouldn't even have to talk about the infield fly rule or when you can run to first on strike three but apparently we do because based on my experience with amateur baseball, it doesn't seem to be sticking.

Let's look at the IFR first, but only briefly and only as a prelude to the discussion about dropped strike threes. The IFR has a lot of juicy stuff I'll discuss in the sections on base running and defense but as far as how it affects the batter, it really doesn't because he is up there trying to do his thing and if he happens to hit into the IFR, well then, he is out. But let's go over the concept as a refresher.

The IFR rule is born out of the righteous idea that it should never benefit you when you do the opposite of what you are supposed to do, in baseball that means catch the flippin' ball! The concept is simple - when the defense has an unfair advantage to turn a double play by not catching a pop-up, the batter is automatically out so the runners have no obligation to advance and be put out; it's an insurance policy for the offense if you will. This is when there are runners **on first and second or bases loaded, and there are less than two outs. The batter is automatically out so if the ball drops uncaught, the runners are not required to advance, which protects them, although of course, they can at the risk of being put out. (**Remember, the IFR is NOT in effect on a bunt attempt. The rules of baseball will not protect the offense when they have executed a poor bunt). The point is to understand why the rule is in place, to protect the runners in a situation that clearly favors the defense. I know most baseball fans understand this and the reason I bring it up is to point out that if you understand the concept of the IFR, then the whole dropped third strike thing should be easy, because it is rooted in the same principal. Allow me to explain...

Technically, **the batter almost always has the right to first base after he either puts the ball in play or suffers a third strike.** You may have noticed the catcher is credited with a put-out after he catches a third strike and that is because there is a nano-second there where the batter technically becomes a runner but is out when the third strike has been secured by the catcher. If it is not caught, his time as a runner is extended beyond that nano-second as he now has the right to run to first. Without any special rules in this case, the batter-runner advancing to first base would force other runners to have to advance, just like on a pop-up that isn't caught if there was no IFR. If this was the case, the most common double play would not be the old 6-4-3, short-to-second-to-first, it would be the incredibly boring 2-6-3 because a runner on first would be forced to advance and the catcher would simply drop the pitch and throw to the shortstop covering second who would relay to first to double up the batter-runner.

Therefore, the easiest way to think about the dropped third strike situation is to think about the IFR. They are both in place to prevent ill-gotten double plays resulting from failure to meet their most basic obligations, catch the ball. In the case of the dropped third strike, I am going to dub thee, "The Infield Strike Rule", ISR. The IFR is not in place when there is only a man on first because a pop-up gives the batter-runner time to get to first so if the ball drops uncaught, the defense will only get one out most likely by forcing the runner at second. With a dropped third strike, the batter-runner doesn't have this same luxury of time, so the ISR is in place in more situations than the IFL: runner on first, first and second, bases loaded, or runners on first and third. That's right, the ISR will be in place any time a runner is on first base and there are less than two outs. **In these cases, when the ISR is in effect and the third strike (swinging or called) is not caught, the batter is automatically out and the runners are not required to advance.**

Both the IFR and ISR are not in effect when there are two outs of course because there is no risk of a double play, so everybody should be running. When the bases are loaded, the easiest thing for the catcher to do when he doesn't catch the 3rd strike cleanly is to pick up the ball and simply step on home because it is a force out on the runner advancing from 3rd. Technically, the catcher could throw to any other base to force any of the runners advancing.

This rule is probably better understood than it appears because kids are taught very early that they are not forced to run when the batter strikes out, everyone knows this. It's almost always the batter who causes confusion in a desperate attempt to try to get on base after striking out…"hey, maybe if I just run down to first nobody will notice I'm out." It reminds me of the "Seinfeld" episode when George Costanza quits his job on Friday and with great regret shows up at work on Monday morning hoping everyone will forget about his major-fail. George didn't slip by the boss and a runner attempting to steal first won't get away with it either. You can't shoot your way out of town one day and show up for brunch the next. In fact running to first in this situation could trip the first domino of bad baseball and cause a runner already on base to advance and be easily put out. A bit of rationalization might allow the batter-runner to think it's a clever move on his part that might induce the catcher to throw the ball past the first baseman but an alert umpire would place all the runners back where they belong because **running the bases after being put out is against the rules and cause for an interference call** which also calls for the runner closest to home to be called out, rare as this is.

So, turning it around from the ISR definition back to the way we all usually think about it, the runner can advance on **a dropped third strike if first base is unoccupied or there are two outs**; see how easy this is. What's all the fuss? Note that a runner attempting to steal second does not free up first for the taking by the batter-runner because at the time of pitch, first base was occupied.

There is another fly in the ointment on this play and that is on a low pitch that might be caught by the catcher on a short hop. We use the term "dropped" but it really means **a pitch cannot hit the ground before caught**. Low pitches, and especially breaking balls down and away, are going away from the umpire and the catcher often blocks his view if he goes down to block the ball. When it's legal to advance, the batter should never hesitate and wait for the call but hustle to first while the umpires figure it out. The plate umpire may look to a base umpire for help but either way he will either signal strike-three and verbalize the batter is out or he will indicate a strike and then another sign, like the safe sign, to indicate the batter is not yet out.

This exact situation blew up in the second round of the American League playoffs in 2005 between the White Sox and Angels in Chicago. Striking out to end the bottom of the ninth with the game tied at 1, White Sox batter AJ Pierzynski thought the low pitch might have skipped off the ground into Angel catcher Josh Paul's glove so he took off for first. Convinced he made the catch for the third out Paul simply rolled the ball out to the mound and made his way to the dugout.

Amidst some confusion, because it looked like plate umpire signaled both strike and out, the umpires eventually ruled it hit the dirt. The video seems to show it was a very close call and indeed caught by Paul but the inning was allowed to continue and the White Sox scored a walk off run to win the game. Who knows what might have happened if the call went the other way because the Angels were ahead in the series 1-0. Had they a chance to win that night and go two up, it would have been a much different series but the White Sox won 4 straight to take it home, 4-1.

The reason I bring this up is to challenge this rule, as I did in the last section regarding the pitch that simply nicks a batter's uniform. The implication here is that the offense gets an opportunity because the defense did not do its job but in fact, scooping up the short hop is a case of the defense going above and beyond...and this seems as wrong to me as awarding the batter first base on a pitch that is just off the strike zone and is caught cleanly but just grazes the batter's uniform. Again citing the foul-tip precedent, I think it would be a much more straightforward and just call to declare, like the foul-tip, that if a third strike is caught cleanly by the catcher, the batter be called out. The White Sox went on to win the World Series in

2005 quite possibly because of a call based on the most miniscule of technicalities that in my mind was inconsequential to the play.

And we're still not done with dropped third strikes as there is another situation that often causes controversy on this play, when the batter walks away. There are two flavors to this and one is pretty simple, the batter swings and misses, sees the ball on the ground and is so disgusted that he whiffed, makes no effort to run so the catcher simply tags him or the umpire signals he is out after a few steps towards his bench.

The second one is the case where the batter did not realize the ball got loose so he takes a few steps towards the dugout and then his teammates start group-freaking and scream at him to run. He will have the deer-in-the-headlights look for a second before he figures it out and begins his mad dash towards first. While this is happening, the catcher is usually scrambling towards the backstop and the plate umpire is turning as well to find the ball.

Unlike the first scenario, where everything is right there in front of the plate in slow motion, in this case the three participants are scattering in all directions so it's not as quick a decision to decide if the runner gave himself up or not. If he makes it safely to first base, the defensive manager will make an argument that the runner should have been called out for abandoning his effort to advance. This might seem as much left up to the umpire's judgment as the decision on a check swing but the major league rule book is much clearer in this scenario and **declares the batter out once he leaves the dirt circle surrounding home plate.** Other rule books might be different (the high school rule says he is not out until he enters the dugout for example) but umpires working all levels usually default to the pro rule possibly opening themselves up to a valid protest by an alert coach.

"BOO!" - Batting Out of Order

Batting out of order in a baseball game is such a rare event it should serve as testimony that writing stuff down on a piece of paper is always a good idea. The simplest of project plans, it only requires each player to know his own name as well as the guy who is in front of him. What could possibly go wrong? Well, if you've ever came home from a mission to the grocery store without the single most important item on the list, let's say, the shrimp for the dinner party you and your spouse were hosting, had you double checked the list while still at the store, you could have fixed the problem, no harm, no foul. Headed straight for the dog house without the shrimp however, it's still a possibility the party can go on and nobody will miss the stupid shrimp. This pretty much sums up how the rules of baseball deal with batting out of order, you might be able to just skip the mistake and move on, allow me to explain.

First, **there is no penalty for not announcing substitutes.** Every now and then in an amateur baseball game, a coach or scorekeeper will lose track of substitutions, not recognize the name and number of the kid at the plate and relay that information to the head coach who will spring out of the dugout and towards the plate as though the umpire were handing out hundred dollar bills. Usually, it's a case of miscommunication between the teams and even if the substitute was never announced, as long as he is otherwise legal, **his entrance in the game is official once he takes his place on the field.** To the disappointment of the defensive coach, no rule has been violated. As unlikely as this would be in a pro game, it holds true there as well so play simply continues with the newly entered substitute (4).

What purpose would it serve to disqualify a legal player because he wasn't announced? Is there an "announcer" position somewhere on the diamond I've been missing all these years?

But let's say the guy in the box is indeed batting out of turn. The defensive coach once again sees free money and will barely be able to contain himself. As soon as the batter steps in the box, he'll call time out and make a bee-line to the plate - thinking about which fine restaurant he'll blow that "hondo" on - because now he is certain he has caught the other team batting out of order. It will be an out and he'll look like a genius, quite possibly snuffing out a rally just with his awareness and presence. "Wrong again Cornelius McGillicuddy!" (Look it up…) **When batting out of order is discovered before the batter has completed the at-bat, *there is no penalty* and it is fixed by replacing the guy at the plate, the *"improper"* batter, with the guy who should be up, the *"proper"* batter.** (It is very important to understand these definitions to follow the ensuing discussion. Also note "The Improper Batter" is a great name for a sports bar.) It could be a full count with the bases loaded and there is still time to fix the mistake and put the right guy up. You see, if there is still time to go back and get the shrimp, all is good and domestic bliss will reign in the house.

The only way batting out of order becomes a violation of the rules, worthy of penalty, is if the illegal at-bat is completed. An alert coach, who's on to an improper batter, must sit patiently and appeal **before the first pitch (or play) on the next hitter**. If he is really clever, he can expedite the situation by ordering an intentional walk and calling time out to appeal once the improper batter has reached first base. Either way, **the penalty for batting out of order is an out and all positive results of the at-bat will be undone, with one exception, a runner who advanced because of a stolen base, wild pitch/passed ball or balk.** This exception makes sense; the batter might be improper, but the runner was proper, and advanced on his own, so it will stand.

There are two caveats to the rule that can cause confusion when fixing the situation however. First, **the improper batter, the guy who seemingly did the wrong thing, is NOT the guy declared out for the rule violation - it's**

the guy who missed his at-bat, the proper batter. This very often leads to the same guy batting twice in a row, which is odd, but is the correct solution. Let's look at the 2013 Giants for an example, as Posey, Pence and Sandoval often bat 3-4-5. Let's say Hunter Pence bats out of order, rather than Buster Posey, and hits a triple driving in Marco Scutaro from first. Remember, the order should be:

3- Buster Posey, 4 - Hunter Pence, 5- Pablo Sandoval

Upon proper appeal, Posey would be called out for missing his at-bat, Pence would come off third and Scutaro would be placed back at first. The order would pick up after the Posey out, so Pence would come up again, only as the proper batter this time. Funny as it seems, it makes sense because, again, it's the guy who *missed* his at-bat who is declared out, not the guy who batted in error.

The second confusing caveat of the batting out of order penalty is that all outs stand on the play but **the batting-out-of-order out, on the proper batter, supersedes an out made by the improper batter.** Using our same example, where Posey misses his turn at-bat, let's say that instead of hitting a triple, this time Pence hits into a 6-4-3 double play. Upon proper appeal, the out at second on Scutaro would stand as the first out, but the out called on Posey for missing his at-bat would override the out Pence made at first base. It wouldn't be a triple play, there would be two outs called and picking up the order after Posey, the proper batter, Pence would come up again with two outs and nobody on base. Just as it makes sense to allow a Scutaro stolen base to stand during the illegal at-bat, because *it did not* have anything to do with the improper batter, it also makes sense to let the Scutaro out at second stand, because *it did* have to do with the improper batter. The defense shouldn't have to lose any extra outs it got while the wrong guy was up.

Realize that **it is not the umpire's job to point out an improper batter** as it is the teams' responsibility to know who should be hitting. What really causes confusion in these situations is when batting out of order is not caught in time. **If an improper batter is not discovered and he finishes his at-bat and no appeal is made before the next pitch, the improper batter's action is legalized so he becomes the proper batter and the order picks up with the guy after him.** Let me repeat this because it is an unusual situation in sports, where chaos becomes rule if not caught in time: the *improper* batter becomes the *proper* batter once a pitch has been made to the next guy. In our example, if not properly appealed, Posey's missed at-bat would become water under the bridge. After seeing Pence hit into a double play, the defensive manager might be happy to have the clean-up hitter out of the way and be one batter closer to the pitcher's spot. If he lets the violation go unchallenged, the first pitch to Pablo Sandoval legalizes Pence's plate appearance, turns the improper batter into the proper batter, and the game would just move on without ever having Posey hit - so what if there's no shrimp, it's still a party! (I did not just call Buster Posey a shrimp fyi.)

Batting out of order can be very difficult to sort out by coaches and umpires on the field because the focus turns to what *should have* happened, so everyone buries their heads in the scorebook. That's fine but you need to start with what actually took place on the field and re-trace events to figure out who the last legal batter was. If you are in the middle of the count, it's simple, figure out who the last guy was...the guy who singled and is on first, so okay, "who's on first?" Oh my, I didn't mean to start up with that routine but you have to get the name of the guy who batted last and then go to the batting order to figure out who should be up. Again, if you are in the middle of the at-bat then it is uncomplicated, figure out who the proper batter is and put him up there with the existing count. If there is no count, the batter who just finished his at-bat is not the last legal batter because he isn't legalized until a pitch is thrown, so you have to go to the hitter before him. "Oh, the guy who flew out to center, who was that? Oscar? Okay, who is after Oscar in the order?" "Jerry. Jerry should have been the last batter." If he was, all is good. If it wasn't, Jerry will be called out and the order will pick up with the guy who is after him in the order, Bob. I know this might be confusing as you read it but the point is, re-trace the action on the field to figure out who was the last legal batter and then go to the book. Doing it the other way will only make things more confusing, trust me.

As unlikely a situation as it is in the majors it is very possible an improper batter could go unnoticed in an amateur baseball game so it opens the door for cheating as the reward for skipping over guys could outweigh the risk of being caught - let me give you an example that should be easy to follow seeing how much you just learned about this rule.

Let say it's late in a game and a team is in the middle of their order. An unscrupulous coach could send the lead-off hitter up, out of order, to try to get back around to his best hitters. Since most coaches don't know there is no penalty until the at-bat is completed, the opposing coach most likely would point it out right away or after the first pitch and the devious coach would simply say with straight face, "oh yeah, our bad, sorry..." and then the umpire will put the 6th guy up like he was supposed to. But here is a sneakier way to do this...send up the last hitter out of order because he might not garner any attention and in fact, the defense might simply breathe a sigh of relief at the notice of a hitter who is probably not a big threat and not think anything of it. If the last guy in the order isn't noticed out of order, the leadoff guy would bat next.

While it's much more likely a lead-off hitter would get everybody's attention, there is a good chance it would take a pitch or two before someone yells "hey, why is the leadoff guy up?!!!"...and by that time, his presence in the box would have been legalized. If they didn't notice the last guy batting out of order, they have a very small window of time, one pitch, to notice the leadoff hitter batting out of order. I'm not suggesting this as a dark strategy, just pointing out that with the onus for policing this on the coaches and scorekeepers, not the officials; the rules have a loophole that allows an illegal action to be legalized after a very short statute of limitations, one pitch. It would definitely be more punitive to call both the proper and improper batter out but these foul ups are usually the result of an innocent miscommunication and not a premeditated effort to cheat, so calling the skipped batter out will suffice.

While it is a rare infraction of the rules, it happened twice in the major leagues in one week during May of 2009. First, Tampa manager Joe Madden incorrectly listed two 3rd baseman on his lineup card and four days later Houston Astros manager Cecil Cooper swapped his usual one/two hitters but gave the plate umpire a lineup card showing his usual order. Madden wound up losing his DH and had to have his pitcher bat third and lo but behold Andy Sonnanstine delivered an RBI double in a Ray's win. Cooper's Astros had to take an out after improper batter Michael Bourn lead off the game with a single and an alert Ken Macha, the Brewers' manager, properly appealed. Since proper batter Kazuo Matsui didn't hit first, he was called out and Michael Bourn, as the two hitter, got to bat again, walked, and came around to score later on in the inning; busy inning for Bourn but that first hit of course was erased from his batting record, it never happened.

Infrequent as these violations are, you would expect to see them more in the National League where you often see confusing "double switches." These mid-game lineup changes involve multiple substitutions designed to put the relief pitcher in a spot in the order that keeps him from coming up for a while. Pitchers of course are traditionally weak hitters, who are usually pinch hit for in a tight game, so a smart "double-switch" will allow a manager to keep a middle-reliever in the game for an inning or two before he has to hit for him. This of course is not an issue in the American League because they employ the "designated hitter." I only bring this up so I can not-

103

so-cleverly transition from the fascinating topic of clerical errors and batting out of order to that hot potato, the designated hitter.

Psych! Let's keep the DH in the on deck circle for a moment. With all this talk about "batters" and "hitters" and ways to get yourself on base or out, there's really no need to discuss the best way to get on base, the standard base hit, because that's "baseball 101". Poor Crash Davis, if only he could have had a few more bloops kick up the chalk, he could have been as big a star as Roy Hobbs - that guy could rake! So far, I hope you agree that I've written this with respect to your baseball knowledge so I don't need to give you that cornball line delivered in that mock Jerry Seinfeld manner, "Why do they call it the foul pole if a ball that hits it is fair? It should be called the fair pole!" True enough but Jerry is better than that, although I can see Kenny Bania doing that right after that lame Ovaltine bit. Okay, so you agree I haven't insulted your baseball intelligence so forgive me when I ask, do you fully understand fair-foul around the bases? You're probably thinking "of course, if a ball bounces over the bag before landing foul, it's fair." You weren't born yesterday so of course that's true. Well, I've heard interpretations of the rules that declare that fair only if it bounces over the back side of the base before landing foul because the rule book says "when bounding to the outfield *past* the base." A ball bouncing foul over the side of the base isn't "past it" but since its fair if it hits any part of the base, the natural conclusion is that it is also a fair ball if it bounces over any part of the base. I'm just pointing out that the language of the rulebook can sometimes cause you to think twice.

So let me ask you another question, at what point does the ball become irrevocably fair? Imagine a high pop-up around first base with a lot of backspin that falls uncaught and then spins foul; when does that become fair? You are probably thinking that if it lands foul before the bag, it's foul but this isn't always the case if the ball initially lands "past" the base. When we think of balls hit past the base we think of grounders but I've seen pop-ups that land past the bag and spin foul in front of the base and technically, these are fair balls. The pro rule book simply says "past the base" and only implies what the high school book say explicitly, that a ball is irrevocably fair once it touches ground beyond an imaginary line from first to third base. Given this, it is quite possible for that spinner to initially hit "beyond" the base but roll foul on the home plate side of the bag. So what about the ball that ricochets off the rubber into foul ground? Well, as you recall from the section one discussion, since the rubber is closer to home than to second, it sits in front of that imaginary line, so it is foul. Now we can turn the page and talk about the DH.

The Designated Hitter

One of my favorite jokes of all time is by comedian Emo Philips and it goes like this:

Once I saw this guy on a bridge about to jump...

I Said "Don't Do It"
He Said "Nobody Loves Me"

I Said "God Loves You. Do You Believe In God?"
He Said "Yes!"

I Said, "Are You A Christian Or A Jew?"
He Said "A Christian"

I Said "Me Too! Protestant or Catholic?"
He Said "Protestant"

I Said "Me Too! What Franchise?"
He Said "Baptist"

I Said "Me Too! Northern Baptist or Southern Baptist?"
He Said "Northern Baptist"

I Said "Me Too! Northern Conservative Baptist or Northern Liberal Baptist?"
He Said "Northern Conservative Baptist"

I Said "Me Too! Northern Conservative Baptist Great Lakes Region or Northern Conservative Baptist Eastern Region?"
He Said, "Northern Conservative Baptist Great Lakes Region"

I Said, "Me Too! Northern Conservative Baptist Great Lakes
Region Council of 1879, or Northern Conservative Baptist Great Lakes
Region of 1912?"
He Said, "Northern Conservative Baptist Great Lakes Region
of 1912"

I Said, "Die Heretic!" And Pushed Him Over...

Emo's little joke brilliantly points out that even with so many commonalities we have the ability to let passionate differences redefine our brothers as rivals. You could rewrite the joke in many ways, one of which would involve two passionate baseball fans and the last question is: "Designated hitter or no designated hitter?" and the guy threatening to jump answers "designated hitter" and Emo pushes him off the bridge... "Die heretic!"

Professional baseball of course is a house divided when it comes to the designated hitter as the rule was adopted by the American League in 1973 but not the National League (5). Let's take a quick look at the rule and how it functions which is a far simpler task than evaluating the pros and cons of it.

The rule itself is a relatively simple concept but the reasons for having it, the details of the rule, and the implications it has for the manager vary greatly from the professional game to the amateur game. The pro DH argument is the idea that weak hitting pitchers stink up the joint so these sub-par hitters are replaced with guys who can hit on average with regular position players. With 750 roster spots in the pros, about half pitchers, half position players, it is a simple statistical improbability that an individual can be *both* one of the best 375 pitchers in the world, and also be one of the best 375 hitters in the world. The same guy can't win the lottery twice so the DH rule simply allows two guys to fill one spot in the lineup, one who pitches and one who hits - it's a job-sharing rule more or less. The disparity between pitchers' ability to hit versus all the other position players increases proportionately as the level of competition increases and goes over the tipping point at the professional level, where the disparity is so noticeable, it affects the game (6). In the amateur game, the DH is more of an effort

106

to give more players an opportunity to participate in the game than to counter some shortcoming, while allowing the kid on the hill to concentrate his energy on the difficult task of pitching.

In the American League, **a DH simply bats in place of the pitcher, and only the pitcher, and does not start the game in the field. The DH must be in the starting lineup and cannot be added mid-game or reinstated after the DH has been removed from the game.** Like pitchers, who must face at least one batter in the game, **the starting DH must stay in the game to face the starting pitcher at least once** so if the DH were pinch hit for his first time up, the pinch hitter would be declared an illegal sub...if it were discovered before the first pitch to the next guy; again, the one-pitch statute of limitations. To my knowledge, in the 40 year history of the DH, no American league team has started a regular season game with the pitcher hitting for himself, but a handful of times per year, use of the DH will be terminated mid-game; it is the elimination of the DH mid-game that usually has baseball fans questioning how the rule works. There are technically 3 ways the DH is eliminated from use mid-game, **the pitcher pinch-hits for the DH, the pitcher moves to another position** on the field (or another position player comes in to pitch), or, the only one that really ever happens, **the DH assumes a position on defense.**

In a typical game, the DH bats in place of the pitcher and all relief pitchers and gets his 4 or 5 at-bats and his work is done. Every now and then however, a manager might find himself running low on players and needs to have the DH go in and play defense. Since **the DH is locked into his spot in the batting order,** such a substitution on defense means **someone has to fill the batting position of the substituted player...it can't be anybody but the pitcher.**

Let me give you an example. I was lucky enough to be at Fenway Park for a game in 1996 that saw future Hall of Fame pitcher Roger Clemens (7) get his first and only regular season at-bat of his 13 year career with the Boston Red Sox. This was a rare treat as it was before interleague play began the following year, which requires AL pitchers to hit when playing games at NL sites.

In this game, the legendary Jose Canseco was batting 4th as the DH, hitting for Clemens. Late in the game, Red Sox manager Kevin Kennedy pinch hit Mike Stanley, his back up catcher, for center fielder and 9th hitter, Milt Cuyler but this meant the skipper needed to rearrange his outfield lest he have his back-up catcher play center field. Kennedy sent Canseco in to play left, shuffled the outfielders and pulled the center fielder and 9th batter out of the game, Stanley. Since Canseco was locked into the 4th spot, as all players are locked into their place in the order, this automatically popped Clemens into the 9th spot.

The simplest way to think about it is that if the DH goes into the field, he "bumps" another player in the batting order out of the game and that spot must be filled by the pitcher, in this case, the 9th hitter and Clemens. The Sox had a safe lead, 9-4, with Clemens on the hill so when his turn to bat came around, Kennedy simply left Clemens in to hit for himself and finish his complete game victory on the hill.

With a big lead, on a cool spring night, the crowd had thinned in the late innings at Fenway but I'm one of those people who never leave a game early because, as I've said about the game of baseball, you never know what you might see. Also, having appreciated every visit to Fenway Park, I never considered myself too old or proper to take advantage of empty seats down low. If you had a chance to sit in the second row behind home plate for an inning or two, at Fenway Park, to watch Roger Clemens pitch, why wouldn't you?

After beating the 7th inning last call, my good friend Greg Fenton and I moved into our new prime seats to milk that last beer when we were shocked to see Roger Clemens move into the on-deck circle in the bottom of the 8th. Nobody in the park noticed the defensive switches that put Clemens in the order but the "Fenway Faithful" sprung to their feet when Clemens stepped into the box. Suited up with borrowed helmet, bat, and elbow gear a la Barry Bonds, Clemens drilled a base hit up the middle, right through pitcher Norm Charlton's legs and the crowd went wild; it's not clear whether it was a "professional-courtesy" fast ball down the middle. Interleague play and a stint in the National League would give Clemens plenty more at-bats the rest of his career (31 for 179 for a .173 BA) but it was the old DH double switch that yielded his one and only at-bat of his historic Red Sox career, and the first regular season hit by a Red Sox pitcher in twenty-four years. (Please make note, this is not the last time you will read about Jose Canseco in this book.)

The DH rule in amateur leagues is not as straight forward as the AL rule, where one guy simply bats for one player. The high school DH rule allows the hitter to hit for any position player, not just the pitcher, and also locks that player into the same spot in the order, meaning that if the DH goes into the field, the non-hitter must also be replaced. The college rule is even more different, in that the non-hitting pitcher is allowed to come back into the game to hit and the non-pitching DH can re-enter the game to pitch. Combined with re-entry rules for starters, it becomes very confusing so I'm not going to cover those details; that's what the actual rule books are for. The most important aspect of the rule to understand is to know when the DH is eliminated during a game and regardless of the variation of the DH rule from association to association, in general, it goes away when the DH goes in to play defense or the pitcher hits or plays another position.

Attempting to make an argument for or against the DH serves no purpose in my mind; you'll sooner find a consensus in that Israel/Palestinian thing. Either way the game will roll along with one-dimensional players in both leagues bucking the tradition of the archetypal baseball player who has all the 5 tools (8) as pitchers are developed with one skill in mind, pitching, and DHs are asked to do only one thing, hit.

There are pros and cons to both sides of course and while it is always exciting to see a weak hitting pitcher get a key hit, I can't say its worth all the other times you see the usually overmatched guy whiff. As curious as a baseball player is who only plays offense, so too is the practice of pitching around a.230 eight hitter to get to a .130 ninth hitter. Is that really "strategy" or just common sense?

Conversely, while it's more exciting when you don't have lulls in the order, the AL game loses some of the baseball's traditional appeal when there are fewer bunts and pitching changes that match wits between managers. When you think about it though, bunting is still legal in the AL and they often use a DH in the NL, they're called pinch hitters, so however you make your argument, your Venn diagram between the 2 styles of play definitely has a large overlapping shaded area making the two leagues more alike than different. Each pitch and the resulting play once the ball is put in play is the same between the leagues so to me the DH affects how you think about each league more than it affects the game itself. Like the aluminum-wood bat debate, there are business issues affecting jobs, branding and sales that mean too much to each side to allow one philosophy to win out over the other any time soon. Like that bat debate, I am going to go out on a limb (made of wood) to say the status quo is here to stay. If anything, the split between the two leagues is good for baseball in the end because it does offer two flavors; the game is so loved, it's not a debate between one product that is good and one that is bad, it's a debate about which is more-better so all the interest and peppery debate is a sort of tide that lifts both boats as the DH/no DH peacefully co-exist.

Catcher in the Way and Other Delays

Everyone sooner or later must leave home and it is no different for the batter. I've covered most of the controversial rulings that can happen in and around the box but I've saved one topic for the transition to the discussion about base runners because it has so much to teach us about the game... catcher's interference.

In general, **the term "interference" is reserved for acts against the defense that hinder their efforts**, by anyone on the offense or near the field, batter, runners, coaches, umpires or spectators and media. The term **"obstruction" is used for any act that illegally impedes the runner** so technically, when the batter swings and makes contact with the catcher's mitt, which is extended too far forward, it is indeed an act of obstruction on the offense but since the pro rule book tags this as "defensive" interference, it has traditionally been referred to as "catcher's interference." I'm not going to attempt to undo baseball tradition but I think this is why fans are often confused by the two terms, but an informed baseball fan must know the difference between "interference" and "obstruction." The catcher doesn't have to make contact with the hitter by the way, if he simply moves forward and is over the plate, too eager to catch a pitch on a squeeze, for example, he has obstructed the hitter by being in the way.

Not only does catcher's interference teach us about terminology, there are elements to this fairly common play that often leave coaches, players and fans in complete confusion. Let me illustrate this by telling a short story, "The sordid tale of catcher's interference and the delayed dead-ball" or "the comedic turned tragic tale of the advancing would-be-hero protected-runner"...

With the speedy pinch runner representing the winning run on second base in extra innings, the batter took a mighty swing and was obstructed by the catcher resulting in a slow roller, aka "the swinging bunt" down the third base line. The third baseman charged the ball and made his best Brooks Robinson effort to bare hand the ball and desperately throw off balance to first but the batter-runner beat it out. With third base vacated by the would be Brooks, the runner from second took a huge turn around third and as an eager young man might, just kept going on the throw to first in a mad dash to catch everyone sleeping and be the hero for the day. The first baseman was wide awake as it turned out and quickly threw home to nail the runner in a very close play at the plate. When the dust settled, the offensive team's coach quickly rushed the plate to ensure the runner would be sent back to third because there was an obvious catcher's interference so he would of course have a choice to accept the penalty, roll back the trouble and keep the rally alive... But sometimes you have to watch out what you wish for, in this case, an aggressive pinch runner, and the result of the play is that the runner is indeed out at the plate and the batter-runner remained at first. So what went wrong?

Catcher's interference is one of the few baseball plays that results in a "delayed dead-ball", where the ruling is applied at the end of the play. The reason many baseball fans think it is an automatic dead-ball and award is because most of the time these violations by the catcher don't produce a ball in play or everyone sees the interference and stops playing and the umpire calls time. Sure, there is a violation but the play is allowed to finish so the baseball action can take precedence if advantageous to the offensive team. This is where the coach's head was but he didn't realize this is the case only to a certain point. The easiest example to understand is that if the batter hits a home run, the interference would be ignored, no harm-no foul. This is just like the case when interference by the batter on a stolen base is ignored when the runner is still thrown out...the infraction didn't prevent the opposing player from doing his job so the play stands.

A more realistic example is that the result of the catcher's interference is a weak ground ball to the second baseman that allows a runner from third to score. In this case, the offensive team might wish to trade the out for the run, you know, the old bird-in-a-hand thing, and **the rules permit the offense to accept the result of the play or take the penalty for obstruction.** They could also opt to take the award and play for the bigger inning and go for the two-in-the-bush, and let **the batter be awarded first base and have all other runners go back to where they were at the time of the infraction (unless attempting to steal, they would be placed on the next base).** But here is the trick with this rule, *if the batter-runner makes it to first base safely AND all other runners advance one base,* **the interference is ignored.** The rules of baseball say that if the batter and all runners advanced, then the interference must not have been a very effective act so the play stands. In our example, once the batter-runner reached first and the runner on second reached third, all bets were off - end-of-story - there was no interference. The lead runner was not protected one inch past third base just as the batter-runner was not protected one inch past first base so they both were free to advance at their own peril…and the peril was real and realized for the lead runner who was thrown out at home. This play occurred in a high school game I umpired and now everyone in attendance knows the story of the catcher's interference and the delayed dead ball.

The delayed dead-ball rulings are reserved for situations where the game is best served by waiting to see what happens, so, as I said earlier, the baseball action can take precedence when it renders the rules violation inconsequential. The full list of this includes:

- Catcher's interference/obstruction with batter
- Interference by batter when attempted put-out is on runner other than at home

- Interference by batter when runner is advancing to home, (other than hitting a throw from the pitcher not in contact with rubber)
- Obstruction on runners (unless the runner is obviously trapped and about to be tagged)
- Defense touching batted or thrown ball with detached equipment (mask or thrown glove)
- Interference with catcher by umpire
- Use of illegal glove
- Coach physically assists a runner

So, let's see what we learned from this discussion:

1. "Interference" usually refers to an act against the defense; "obstruction" is an act against the batter and/or runner.
2. A ball put in play on catcher's interference is live so the batter-runner should run hard out of the box as always.
3. All runners are protected for advance to the next base only.
4. The offense has the option of accepting the result of the play and ignoring the interference or accepting the award, batter-runner goes to first and all runners return (except those advancing in a steal attempt at time of pitch).

Part II Footnotes

(1) Check out former major leaguer Wally Bachman's exploits as a minor league manager on Youtube and you'll see what I mean.

(2) I use the term "sport" loosely. I think of golf as more of a game than a sport, like darts. A sport is supposed to demonstrate an athletic challenge amongst rivals and there is no way a 72 year guy should be able to beat a 25 year old in a sport. Go find me a thousand 25 years olds and see if one of them can beat Jack Nicklaus in a golf match and if they can't, give them a year of lessons and free rounds and see if they can do it when he is another year older.

(3) Pro rule, most amateur leagues that allow wood bats also allow composites which are made of multiple pieces of wood which are designed to be more durable.

(4) Many amateur leagues have rules permitting starters to be removed and re-entered into the game once or other rules designed to allow for maximum participation by all players. Also, not all designated hitter rules are equal so local rules should be carefully scrutinized.

(5) The idea of the DH had been kicking around since 1906, the days of Connie Mack, and was championed in the early 1970s by colorful Oakland A's owner Charlie Finley. The use of it was adopted by the AL before the 1973 season but rejected by NL owners.

(6) Examples: Pitchers exclusively hit last in the order, often are called on to bunt in non-traditional situations (with one out), and are often forced up by the defense pitching around the 8th hitter. NL pitchers collectively hit around a buck forty each year. Nuff said.

(7) Yes, "future", sooner or later, Roger Clemens will win election to the Hall.

(8) Ability to 1-hit for average, 2- hit for power, 3- speed on the bases, 4- fielding skills, and 5- a strong arm

The Rules Abide!

Part III – The Runner

Rite of Passage

If you've ever watched little kids run around the bases on an otherwise empty baseball diamond, you'll notice it's with an air of pure joy. They might be too young to know much about the game of baseball but somehow they've absorbed the idea that making it all the way to home is a good thing; something deep inside them lets them feel good about crossing the plate at full speed.

I've been making the argument that baseball is a grand metaphor for American life because opportunity abounds and life is but a trip around the bases so to speak. As innocent children, we're eager to run as fast as we can, blind to the ways of the world that can trip us up along the way, but as we live and learn and gain a better understanding of how things really work, we slowly equip ourselves with the knowledge and wisdom to carve out our own path and enjoy the journey.

More often than not, success doesn't come quickly but methodically, one stage or step at a time in the progression to reach an important end-goal. This is what makes the home run so exciting in baseball, that in one fell swoop, we can earn a free pass through the obstacles, all our enemies at ease while we parade, unfettered at our leisure, knowing we will arrive at our goal into the welcoming open arms of our brothers. This is why the home run, more than anything else in sports, is so transcendent, and at the same time so elusive, because in reality, life offers very few chances where we can succeed so dramatically and abruptly and it's unclear that we all have the ability to do so. In fact, there are very few people blessed with skills that allow them to dominate the game, baseball or life, so more often than not brains will trump brawn at the end of the day – I'm talking about our own brains versus our own brawn.

Okay, now I'm just talking about baseball and specifically about base running and the point I am trying to make is that home runs are fine but most runs are scored one base at a time so base running skills are a very important and overlooked part of the game. As exciting as a homerun is, that appears in an instant, running into outs on the bases has an equal and opposite affect on the game, disheartening and draining, also in an instant. Speed is a good tool in the right hands but without care, it's nothing but unrealized potential.

I used to play adult ball with a guy whose nickname was "Suicide" because of his great ability to run into outs on the bases, almost pathologically. I could never quite put my finger on it but obviously there was a lack of awareness going on that killed one rally after another — it drove everyone crazy. Good decision making on the bases involves a lot of calculations and risk management that can only be based on a deep level of awareness of the game itself, one's own ability and the situation at hand. On top of all that, it really helps if you have a good understanding of the rules too. In this section, we're going to look at the often misunderstood rules of baseball as they impact the runner's trip around the bases, both positively and negatively. You can't necessarily teach baseball instincts but there should be no excuse for not knowing the rules...so let's touch 'em all and remember, life is but a journey.

Right of Way

As soon as the batter's business is done in the box, he becomes a runner with the right to advance. The most fundamental responsibility for the runner is not to interfere with the defense as he moves from station to station. Interference can occur in a number of ways which I'll explore as we move around the bases but the most basic and common conflict of interest occurs when the runner's path to the next base crosses paths with the fielder's path to the ball. Base runners think the game is all about them and their right to advance but **the fielder has the right of way when making a play on a batted ball**...I repeat, the fielder has the right of way to field a batted ball. I didn't say the fielder always has the right of way, as in "all the time, 24-7"; the key language is "on a batted ball." In general, the rules protect everyone's right to do their job, that is, pitchers pitch, hitters hit, runners run and fielders field. I know, a brilliant statement so call me "Captain Obvious" when I say that the rules abide if anyone gets in the way of any of those actions. If the runner cuts off the fielder and **creates contact or causes any hindrance – a double pump, a stutter step, any interruption of their effort - the runner risks being called out for interference** and it may be worse: **a second out can also be called if the interference prevented an additional out**. It gets worse still as **remaining runners must go back to where they were at the time of pitch.** The offense is not allowed to make any advance on a play where they've broken the rules.

There is one very important caveat about this whole right of way scenario, the fielder has the right of way on his initial attempt at the ball but if he boots it, all bets may be off. The idea is that the fielder must have a fair chance to make the play but once he has had that chance, and failed, **the fielder is not necessarily protected beyond that first touch.** Any contact that may occur between the runner and fielder, or additional fielder that comes into the play, beyond that, is probably incidental and should be ignored...however there is an exception to this exception in the interpretation of the rules. A ball that is clearly misplayed is one thing, but sometimes a fielder makes a nice play to block a hot shot and keep the ball in front of him so **his continued action on the play, to pick up the ball and make a throw, should still be protected if the ball is within his immediate reach**. The bottom line for runners is they should not only avoid contact with fielders but give them plenty of room, in order to avoid any risk of a an interference call and the resulting penalties.

I mentioned that a second out can be called when the interference prevents a double play. The most common example of this in amateur baseball, especially in high school, is when there is an illegal slide to break up a double play turn at second; **the runner is called out and also the batter-runner. Interference does not have to be intentional** but if it is, there is a specific statement in the rule book that says **if the runner "deliberately and willfully" interferes in an obvious attempt to break up a double play, he will be called out but the second out will not necessarily be the batter-runner, but the runner closest to home plate**. If the bases were loaded with no outs and a ball was hit to the shortstop and the runner from second intentionally let himself be hit by the ball, he would be out for interfering as well as the runner on third so the batter-runner would be allowed first base, forcing the runner on first up to second base.

Case Study: "It Happened Right There!"

When we conjure up interference scenarios we tend to think about stuff that happens in the middle of the diamond but the batter turns into a runner right there in the batter's box and that's where his responsibility to yield begins. While I've seen runners interfere with pitchers crossing into the first base foul line to catch a pop-up, it could happen even sooner than that, like on the first step out of the batter's box! Let's go to the "Way-Back Machine" and look at a play that had a big impact in the 1975 World Series, won by the "Big-Red Machine", The Cincinnati Reds. I'm sure you think of Carlton Fisk's walk-off home run when you think of the '75 World Series, the famous shot off the left field foul pole at Fenway in the 12th inning of game six, winning the epic game and forcing a deciding game seven. The image of Fisk waving it fair as he hopped down the first base line is burned into our minds as the signature moment of one of the greatest World Series of all time but there were many other great moments in that series' legacy. There were other dramatic homers (Bernie Carbo's pinch-hit shot to tie game six in the 8th, Tony Perez' monster clearing moon shot off

Bill Lee's eephus pitch (1) to get the Reds back in game seven), the games were tight (five one-run games), both teams played great defense and on top of all that, the series followed the Oakland A's three-peat from '72-'74, so there was great interest nationally in seeing two emerging teams face off to see who would be the new champion. Talent indeed, as the series featured:

- Five future Hall of Famers (Johnny Bench, Tony Perez, Joe Morgan, Carl Yastrzemski, Carlton Fisk).
- One injured future Hall of Famer (Jim Rice).
- One still-future Hall of Famer (Pete Rose).
- One very rare, dual Rookie of the Year & MVP (Fred Lynn).
- Other greats like Luis Tiant and Ken Griffey, Sr., as well as outfielders George Foster and Dwight Evans who racked up 733 career home run between them.

By the way, Fisk's game-six clincher was just a little sweeter for anybody lucky enough to be sitting on a ticket for game seven and that included me. Down by three runs in the 8th, the heartbreak was setting in for the loss and the personal near-miss. The story to get that ticket is a good one as it required skipping school and standing in line for eight hours, the old fashioned way, but when we finally made it to the ticket window and all that was left were SRO tickets for game 7, my buddies Brian, Rick and I figured there was no chance in the world the upstart Sox would take the Reds to the limit. Fisk's game winner not only completed a great comeback, it guaranteed a 15 year old kid a trip to a World Series game 7. It doesn't matter that the bad guys won, I still cherish that ticket stub, face value six bucks.

I have to tell you about one other added benefit from attending game 7. Since ballpark security wasn't as tight as it is today, despite the home team losing the game, the crowd still spilled on to the field following the final out, in some cathartic attempt to prolong the experience and magical season. I just

121

couldn't pass up the chance so I entered the field over the short right field fence down in the corner and worked my way around the field, going to every position on the diamond. The mound was tricky as there was a mounted Boston cop patrolling the infield but eventually I went to all 9 spots on the diamond and imagined what it would be like to play baseball at Fenway Park, literally, a once-in-a-lifetime opportunity.

Okay, history lesson over, my original point is that while everyone remembers Fisk's moment of glory, The Sox catcher was involved in another iconic moment in that series, a potential interference call that produced one of the most controversial plays in World Series history. With the series tied one game apiece and game three tied 5-5 in the 10th inning, Cincinnati Reds reserve outfielder Ed Armbrister was sent up to the plate to lay down a sacrifice bunt following a leadoff single by Cesar Geronimo. On a 1-0 pitch, Armbrister topped a sinker by Red Sox reliever Jim Willoughby and bounced a bunt high in front of the plate. As he took his first step out of the box towards first, Fisk rushed forward and collided with Armbrister as he reached for the ball. If we stop the imagined video right here, what do we have? Text book interference because the runner "failed to avoid the fielder" and there was no doubt that there was contact with the fielder by the runner. I'm sure you're thinking, "of course he thinks it was interference because he's a Red Sox fan still scarred from '75 Series"...and that might be true but read on. (You can see the picture of the contact at www.TheRulesAbide.com)

So we have a fielder who seemingly was impeded in an attempt to field a batted ball, because there was contact, right there, three feet in front of the plate. If we roll the video forward for another second, we'll see that while there was a "collision", it was more of a fender-bender at best as Armbrister, a 160 pound native Bahamian, bounced off the lumberjack sized catcher, at six foot three. If you look at the video closely, Armbrister actually makes a slight move to duck out of the way just as he steps, however slightly, in Fisk's way but regardless, the catcher cleanly fielded the ball and quickly fired to second in an attempt to force out Geronimo, although he could have as easily tagged out Armbrister right there on the spot for the sure out. The throw to second was high however and sailed into center field. Geronimo slid safely into third ahead of a sweet Fred Lynn throw and Armbrister, believe it or not, wound up on second base so now there was still nobody out and the Sox were in trouble. Let's review; in that first instant, it appeared to be interference and I will argue "is" interference but in that second instant, Fisk, albeit slightly delayed, fielded the ball successfully. While you can argue the fielder rushed the throw because of the lost second due to the contact with the batter-runner, it is difficult to argue the throwing error was caused by Armbrister, as Fisk cleanly fielded the ball and made a throw in an uninterrupted motion. As difficult as it is to admit, a good throw would have easily beat Geronimo to second.

I've presented a handful of facts about the play in my analysis but the action itself only took about 2 seconds and in the heat of the moment, home plate umpire Larry Barnett ruled that there was no interference. This was an unusual interference situation because the runner and fielder usually start off far out of each other's way but in this case, I guess you could say God put the runner in the way because the catcher naturally is behind the batter at the time of the pitch. This is an important point, but all other analysis aside, in a decision making moment, umpires often ask themselves, who behaved badly or did something wrong on the play. In this case you can argue nobody did, the runner did what he was suppose to, as did the catcher. Given it happened so fast and clearly wasn't flagrant, Barnett ruled it was simply a baseball play with incidental contact. As I mentioned earlier, the rule book explicitly states that **interference does not have to be an intentional act** by the runner.

Red Sox skipper Darrel Johnson rushed Barnett and a lengthy argument ensued. Johnson was furious, begging for help from the first base umpire and yelling to Barnett that the "runner was all over him." An exasperated Barnett snapped back "I can't help that, it happened right there" pointing to the batter's box. Johnson didn't give up his argument but having never brought Barnett's mother into the discussion, was not ejected and when the dust settled and the game resumed, Joe Morgan quickly took care of business and singled Geronimo home with the winning run. Had interference been called, there would have been one out, Geronimo would have been put back on first, and the Reds would have had to sacrifice with an out or risk an inning ending double play. Pete Rose could have hit a home run as well so we will never know what would have happened, only that the non-call played a role in the Reds going up 2-1 in the series they would take home, 4 games to 3 about a week later.

This is a fantastic case study that demonstrates that not all calls in baseball are as black and white as safe-out or fair-foul. There were a lot of forces to be reckoned with, the intentions of the players, the spirit vs. the letter of the rules, context in the enormity of the World Series and extra innings and umpire judgment as well. Barnett let the baseball action take precedence and had Fisk made a good throw, Geronimo would have been out and the play would have been as unmemorable as Ed Armbrister's baseball career (2).

At the same time it wasn't outside the realm of possibility that the Red Sox could have turned a double play and Reds' manager Sparky Anderson might very well have found himself arguing for an obstruction call on Fisk who slightly tripped Armbrister on his way to first. Decades later, bitter Red's fans might still lament the call that helped them lose the series to Boston.

If we fast forward back to the future, we can see that a special comment was added to the rule book that specifically says **contact, when the catcher is fielding the ball, in general, is no violation and nothing should be called**. This special note was added before the 1976 season and is obviously a clarification based on the Fisk-Armbrister play. Remarkably, if you listen closely to the on field argument, which was being recorded for TV, Barnett indeed makes this point several times to Johnson, who of course was having none of it, "When the batter comes out of the box after hitting the ball and the catcher makes a play, there is no interference." Barnett not only called the play correctly but quoted the rules. I mentioned earlier that God, or Alexander Cartwright I suppose, placed the batter-runner and the catcher so close together at the plate that an exception to the interference rule is necessary there. This doesn't mean any intentional act or flagrant interference or obstruction is allowed near the plate, only that it is very possible for slight contact in such close quarters to happen and it should be ruled as incidental and legal.

The Running Lane, "Yeah...No!"

If a batter turned runner can avoid trouble getting out of the box, there's a trap waiting for him the second half of that run toward first, when he reaches the running lane, **a three foot wide box that starts halfway up the first base line at the 45 foot mark and ends at the base.** The three feet of running space is mostly in foul ground although **the foul line itself is the inside boundary of the lane,** which exists whether chalked or not.

The purpose of the running lane is to keep the runner on a straight and narrow path to the base and out of the way of a throw from fair territory. That all looks good on paper but we know from watching baseball games that it never stops the runner from running in fair territory in order to draw a bad throw over his shoulder on a bunt or chopper in front of the plate. The batter-runner is responsible for keeping both feet within the box so if he is straddling the foul line, **one foot in, one foot out, he is not legal** and remember, it's only the last 45 feet that matters.

Although many runners don't pay attention to the lane, the reason you hardly ever see a runner called out for a violation is because **simply running outside the lane is not cause for punishment, the runner actually has to interfere with the throw or a fielder to be called out.** Major leaguers are pretty good at this baseball thing so you won't see too many bad throws on these routine plays and even at the amateur level it doesn't happen too often.

The primary responsibility for calling this is the home plate umpire as he is looking up the line and in fact often gaining ground not far behind the runner to keep an eye on a number of things, which we'll discuss later in the umpire section, including the running lane violation. If the runner is hit by a throw and is out of the lane, in general he should be called out. If he is running outside the lane and suddenly zigs back in and is hit you have a trickier situation but an alert umpire should recognize an effort to confuse the defense and call interference. These are routine and easy to call as infrequently as they happen.

The situation that really causes coaches fits is when the runner is outside the lane and there is a bad throw but there is no interference call. As we will see in our trek around the bases, the runner more or less defines his own path and the onus is always on the defense to make an accurate throw. Very often a runner is outside the lane when a poor throw to first goes down the right field line and a coach will come out of the dugout begging for an out to be called. The rules of baseball are written so that the burden of proof is on the player before an award is made on technical violation so again, the baseball play should take precedence over a seemingly inconsequential rules violation. If the runner interferes with a good throw, that is certainly a violation but if the fielder makes a bad throw while the runner is out of the lane, well then, it's nothing more than a bad throw, and an error. The coach will argue the runner caused the bad throw and that is something the umpire should consider but simply running outside the lane is not cause for an interference call by itself. I suppose the catcher has the option of drilling the runner in the back with a throw when he sees him running on the inside, but there is never any guarantee an umpire will call interference, although he should.

One last thing about running to first base, remember that it's the runner's responsibility to give way to a fielder so **it is okay for the runner to leave the running lane when doing so to allow a fielder access to a ball** that is dribbling up the first base line. If that runner was subsequently hit by a throw outside the lane he would not necessarily be called out because he initially did what the rules called for.

Trouble at the Turn

The best part of beating out a close call at first base is the freedom to run through the base (or slide) as though you just won a 100 yard dash — you slow down as you bundle up the finish line ribbon that is gathered around your midsection. The umpire calls out an enthusiastic "safe" and you're free to relax for a moment to catch your breath as you stroll back to the base, protected by the rules from being put out by the first baseman.

Then there's a different situation - just as the runner feels that first rush of accomplishment, he realizes a throw from the infielder sailed over the first baseman's head and there is another rush of adrenaline as the runner's brain works overtime...

> "OMG it's a bad throw!...I'm going to go to second...no wait, it bounced off the fence and there is no way I can make it so I better stay here....stay calm...walk slowly back to first so you don't make it look like you turned and headed to second...."

Yes, in a second about 3 or 4 things went through the runner's mind and if he so much as looked towards second, the defensive team will be calling for the first baseman to tag him out on his way back to first base.

Rule books vary but in general they only go as far as saying the runner **is available for put out if he makes an "attempt" to run towards second**, some books say "feint" as well. This is another example, not unlike begging for balks, where one team is calling on the other team to pay a pretty big price for a small movement; in this case, the defensive team wants an out to be called on a guy who just earned his way to first, taking them off the hook for letting that happen. Like the check swing, **it is a judgment call whether or not the runner made an attempt**. You could say an initial movement towards second is like the initial effort on the check swing when the batter moves the bat somewhat forward. After that, it is a question of did he actually strike at the ball and in this case, did he actually attempt to go to second? In my opinion, he has to go beyond that first instinctive flinch and make it an unquestionable effort to try to stretch it to two…but that's just me; someone else might declare any movement other than running directly down the right field line as an effort.

The key for a coach to argue this is to pin the umpires in the corner with the question, "did he make an attempt towards second." The best way to "argue" any call is to use the parlance of the rule book when possible. Also, the rule book says **the runner cannot leave the baseline after touching first base** so the right to overrun the base is not a free pass to go hang out, he must return immediately. Think of this just as the move to second, only the opposite direction, towards the dugout. If the runner appears to head there because he thinks there are three outs for example, he can be called out for "abandoning." I hope you never see this one but I've seen it called in the pros, just this summer, on Jacoby Ellsbury of the Red Sox, who started towards the dugout after overrunning first base, thinking his fielder's choice at second was the third out. And one more thing for coaches, remind your kids they **don't have the right to overrun first base on a walk**; just like the case where Johnny can't read, some kids get all the way to high school not knowing this.

Interference, On the Ball

My first example of interference was around the plate but it's much more common to see this as runners move from first to third and cause trouble for the middle infielders. It's common to see a runner take a stutter step to avoid being hit by a ball and runners need to think of the defensive players just as they think about the ball, because they can't get in their way either. If there is any contact with the fielder before he makes an attempt on the play, interference will be called if it is deemed the fielder had a reasonable chance to make a play. Too often the runners are looking at the ball and not the second baseman charging in to field it and I've seen a number of collisions that result in injury to one or both players on top of the runner being called out.

I said earlier, interference can come in a number of forms and the most obvious one is a runner being hit by a batted ball.

We've all seen a hot shot towards short clip a too-clever-for-his-own-good-trying-to-screen-the-fielder runner; time is called, "Einstein" is called out and the batter is placed on first (a second out can be called if it prevented an attempt on a double play). That is how it usually goes down but what about this scenario: a runner is on third base and a chopper is hit down the third base line – the third baseman charges in and towards the line but misses the backhanded attempt on the short-hop.

The runner, who went back to third is standing on the base, is hit squarely in the back by the bounding fair ball. Is he out? Obviously, from the set-up, you know the answer is that the runner is NOT out because he was protected by being on the base right? No – not right – that is the trick part of the question. **The only time a runner is protected from**

being called out when hit and on a base is on the infield fly rule. No, the runner on third who is hit is not out because he did not interfere with the fielder's attempt to make a play. My whole life I thought being hit by a batted ball was the infraction but it's not; the infraction is "interfering" with a fielder. Once you think about it like that it becomes crystal clear.

In the hot-shot to short example, the runner denied the fielder the opportunity to get the job done and thus has "interfered." **Once the ball has passed any infielder (except the pitcher) or touched any infielder (including the pitcher) the runner should not be called out when accidentally hit by the batted ball, provided another fielder doesn't have a chance to also make a play.** Let's say a ball was hit in the hole and it got past the diving third baseman but hit the runner advancing to third, he should be called out because the shortstop still could have made a play, if he was moving that way of course.

But let's look at a bases loaded situation and the infield is drawn in; a hot-shot anywhere hits one of the runners on the dirt while all the infielders are in on the grass – THAT BALL IS LIVE! I'm not sure why we don't see this more often but when it does happen, all hell will break loose because everyone will think the ball is dead and stop and then the umpires will have a genuine situation on their hands. I haven't seen it personally but I would just give a safe sign and yell out "ball is live!" to keep the action going. Also, it is not the umpire's judgment that a fielder could have made a successful play that is important, just that he had a chance, any chance, to field the ball. The shortstop might have no chance at first on the ball in the hole but by cutting it off, he could prevent the runner from rounding third and scoring so it's not about the batter, it's about possession of the ball and opportunity to play it.

One more thing about the guy hit while on the base; it bears repeating that a runner has no immunity from an interference call while he is standing on a base, except on an

IFR situation, so he must know his responsibilities. As I've been saying all along, the runner must allow a fielder the chance to make the play so if he sees the ball coming his way he obviously can't touch the ball but he also can't puff himself up either to make it difficult for the fielder. He doesn't have to leave the base but he has to make an effort to get out of the way, even on an IFR.

This situation with the runner being hit also applies to any interference by the umpires if they are hit by a batted ball. **If the umpire is hit before a fielder has an attempt to make a play (again, we don't count the pitcher), then the ball is immediately dead.** The umpire is a neutral party of course (no jokes please) so we cannot penalize the offense and we also have to protect the defense as best we can so **the runner is awarded first base and all runners must go back;** in theory, everyone gets a little somethin-somethin. I remember working the plate in a high school game in San Diego where my partner was hit on a sharp ball to the right side in a first and third situation. I immediately called time and pointed the runner advancing home back to third and put the batter on first and the next thing I knew my partner and I were being heckled by both sets of parents. The hitting team's fans were riled up that the runner was not allowed to score and the defensive team's fans were ticked off because the ball was headed straight for the second baseman and a presumed out or double play. "Book rule" was applied, yet it was viewed that both teams had something taken away, not given. Perspective is everything I suppose but the ire was born out of ignorance of the rules and lack of understanding that justice was equally served.

Just as with a ball that hits a runner, **if the ball strikes the umpire behind the infielders, it is still a live ball.** Again, a hot-shot with the infield pulled in or a rocket past the first baseman that gets Blue on the line behind first are the top candidates for this one, but it's easier to administer since it doesn't involve the players; the umpire will simply indicate the ball is still in play by extending his arms out as in the "safe" sign. Also, while we are on the subject of umpires causing havoc, note that if the umpire interferes with the catcher as he attempts to put out a runner who is stealing, and the throw is not successful, it is considered interference. **The result is a delayed dead ball. If the throw is not successful, time is called, the runner must go back.**

Infield Fly Rule Part II – The Runners

The discussion about the infield fly rule and the runners' responsibilities should be brief but I am always surprised to see players surprised when the IFR is called and all hell breaks loose once the ball hits the ground. It takes but one clown to trip the first insane-base-running domino and all of a sudden, it seems like the circus is in town and the diamond is the center ring. Everyone involved with a baseball team should not only know the IFR, but recognize when it's a possibility, in real-time, during games so there is no panic if the ball indeed is not caught. If you pay attention to the officials, you'll notice they signal each other before each batter and they have a special sign when the IFR is in effect. Using either the index finger to indicate one out or the open hand, palm facing in, to indicate no outs, the home plate umpire will touch the brim of his cap and the base umpire(s) will return the same sign to acknowledge. If the officials have a plan in place to remind themselves, certainly the base coaches should as well, so every runner knows to recognize the potential for the call and alertly watch the umpires who will point to the sky and call out "infield fly rule." If base coaches can be programmed to yell "make sure he goes home" on every 3-2, two out situation, surely they can dish out a little love when the IFR is in effect. Umpires are largely invisible to the players during the action but this is a situation where they need to be trained to break baseball's fourth wall and look to the umpires for their call or non-call. Know the rule – recognize the situation – look for the call!

Speaking of the IFR, I mentioned in the previous section about interference that **the only time a runner is protected by being on the base, and being hit, is in an IFR** situation but if the base runner were to wander off the base and be hit by the pop-up, it doesn't matter that the batter is already out, the runner would be out too. File this in the "never-in-my-lifetime" folder.

Three Men on a Base

There are two other ways for a runner to find an out when they lose sense of themselves on the base paths, overtaking another runner or sharing a base. The first situation usually happens when there is a ball deep in the outfield that may or may not be caught and the lead runner hesitates while the trailing runner is charging full speed ahead, especially if the lead runner stays on first to tag up. I've also seen the lead guy, who thought the ball was caught, but wasn't, race back to first and come face to face with the batter-runner rounding first and digging hard for second. **Anytime one runner passes another, the trailing runner is out and the ball is live.** The umpires should call it in real time as though the player was tagged out by pointing and signaling an out. Keep in mind the trailing runner has to clearly pass the lead runner so if they are side-by-side, they are good and also, if one of the runners happen to throw an arm out to physically stop the other guy, this is okay too, it's only the base coaches that cannot physically assist the runner (a delayed ball out).

Additionally, tag ups are discussed in this book in a number of contexts, so this is as good a place as any to point out that **the runner is free to leave his base the instant the fielder first touches the ball**. He does not have to wait until the continued action of the fielder is complete and/or he has demonstrated control of the ball, following a juggle perhaps. I'll elaborate more on what makes a catch in the section on defense but keep in mind the runner only needs to time his break with the fielder's first touch of the ball.

Occasionally you'll see a situation where two runners find themselves on the same base and it's usually after some degree of base running blunder and the runners are smart enough to stick together to avoid a double play. That's the vanilla flavored version but it's possible for three runners to end up on one base and it actually happened once in the major leagues. I had the pleasure of meeting a gentleman who proudly told me about his grandfather, Dazzy Vance, a Hall of Fame pitcher, class of '55. I had heard of Dizzy Dean but never Dazzy Vance and a little homework revealed that Vance was one of baseball's prototypical power pitchers, dominating the National League in the 1920s as he led the league in strike outs seven consecutive years with the Brooklyn Dodgers. Famous for his fastball, his legend was born because of his slow feet after taking part in one of the most famous baseball bloopers in major league history...3 men on a base.

It happened in a 1926 game vs. the Boston Braves. Vance was on second base, Chuck Fewster on first when Babe Herman hit a long ball deep to right. Vance initially held up thinking the ball might be caught so he got a very late break but both Fewster and Herman read it correctly as a ball that was going to hit off the right field wall. As the slow footed Vance rounded third, the base coach put up the stop sign for Fewster behind him but Vance thought it was for him so he stopped and went back to the third base bag (occupant #1) as Fewster rolled in a moment later (#2). Herman, thinking triple all the way never looked up after the carom off the wall and must have had a precious look on his face when he arrived at the team meeting at third base (#3)...and then what? All three players stayed on the base so the Braves third baseman tagged them all just to be safe. By rule of course Dazzy, the first one on the scene, was safe while Fewster and Herman were called out. **In a non-force situation, he who gets there first owns the base. Obviously if a runner is forced and does not advance**

he loses his right to that base so the guy coming up behind him is protected from being put out once on the bag. In this case Babe Herman essentially doubled into a double play. Obviously the best thing for the runners to do is stay on the base to keep a bad situation from getting worse. Note that I said he "who gets there first" owns the base which is just my way of saying the preceding runner has the right to the base. It's possible in a rundown that a runner goes back to a base already occupied, so it looks like he is the second guy to the base, but as the lead runner who already passed that base, he is considered to have acquired it first.

Getting There From Here, the Baseline

While we're on the subject of running the bases, let's take a look at one of the more argued aspects of getting from point A to point B, running out of the baseline. The most common misconception about this is that the runner has to follow a certain line around the bases, but have you ever seen a guy called out, after hitting a home run, for taking a long wide run around the diamond? Of course not. As long as he touches all the bases and in the proper order, there are no restrictions on exactly where he runs. When you think about it - we just talked about the first base running lane - if there was a predetermined path, there would be a running lane all the way around the bases and of course there is not. Other than that second half of the way to first base the runner is free to choose his own path. That's right, you read this correctly.

We've all seen a poor base runner take a big wide turn around a base and all it does is increase his chance of being thrown out at the next stop. Since there is no advantage to running wide, it is legal...except when running to avoid a tag. In this aspect, the common idea of running out of the baseline is correct but what is often overlooked is that **the bases don't determine the baseline, the runner does.**

135

The baseline is established as a direct line from the runner to the next base at the time a fielder is attempting a tag and the runner is allowed 3 feet on either side of that. Three feet is not much, about a step and a walking one at that, but there are several reasons why this is not such an easy call. First, the player is moving in two directions; he is running hard towards the base but also drifting sideways to avoid a tag. Since he can cover five or six feet in one stride toward the base, the line that must be measured is a diagonal one, starting from where he was a step ago, so this measurement requires evaluating two planes of a fast moving object. Officials like to be precise which is difficult in these situations so an umpire is only going to make this call if he is absolutely sure it is more than a 3 foot deviation. It's not unlike a cop writing speeding tickets and why you know that when the speed limit is 55, it really means 65. You have to be obviously speeding to warrant a ticket and the runner must be obviously "out of the baseline."

The second factor that buys the runner more benefit of the doubt is that since the runner's job is to avoid the fielders and, by most amateur rule books, the runner is required to avoid a fielder trying to tag him, the first sideways step before reaching the fielder re-establishes his position before the tag attempt and re-establishes the baseline. In this light, running out of the baseline is not measured in feet but typically in steps, not unlike the two steps you are allowed in basketball without dribbling while attempting a layup. The disconnect, and the reason for so many arguments, is that the defensive coach is thinking 3 small feet, 36 inches, but in practicality, an out will not be called until there is a third step to avoid a tag which is going to take him 5-6 feet sideways. This is why you never see a marginal out-of-the-baseline call argued by the offense, they are only called when it is obvious so the argument is usually by the defense after a non-call when the runner made a narrow escape with those two strides.

The rules also refer to this thing called "abandoning" the bases which is a penalty more for being a bonehead and not knowing the situation rather than for making an illegal baseball play. The rule book mentions it mostly in the context of not returning to first base immediately after over running or over sliding the base. I wouldn't have thought this had been called in the history of the game, until I saw the Ellsbury play. A more realistic example is that after a "walk-off" hit that produces the winning run, trailing runners don't touch their next base, in theory allowing them to be forced out, or perhaps a runner thinks he was out at first and peels off towards the dugout. These runners can be called out but in my opinion, the officials should do everything they can to avoid doing so as they are pure technical rule violations and don't have much to do with actual play.

Another obscure rule violation is **running the bases in reverse, which calls for a dead ball and the runner being declared out. This only applies to an effort to run the bases backwards to confuse the defense, not when rule requires it.** An example of this would be a first and third situation when the runner from first steals and the defense is indifferent so upon arriving at second base, the runner retreats towards first to try to draw a throw and get in a pickle, a common practice in the games early years which, in fact, got its name from 1920's Cleveland outfielder George Gerken. Nicknamed "Pickles", he was especially good at drawing throws and then escaping tag outs motivated mostly by side bets from teammates. Beyond the baseball meaning, when they couldn't pay up, it was common to hear "I'm in to Pickles…" which later evolved to people saying "I'm in a pickle" when owing money or being trapped between bases. George "Pickles" Gerken was real but I have to say the story isn't and is as ridiculous as running the bases backwards.

Slide Show

A crash at the plate in a baseball game can in one moment be the most exciting play in sports and the next moment turn gruesome like when Giant's catcher Buster Posey's left leg snapped under the pummeling by the Marlin's Scott Cousins in 2011. Such train wrecks are the stuff of professional baseball, justified because so much is at stake when the game is played by the big boys: championships, legacy, money, fame, et al. Traditionally, lowering a shoulder is as hardball as hardball gets but as much as we admire fearless and tough players, exposing a defenseless catcher to such a free shot seems inconsistent with the very nature of baseball because it's simply not a showcase for brute force...which is nothing more than my opinion. That said, this play is legal in professional baseball but not in any amateur league I know. This has to be the biggest difference between pro and amateur rules and requires a serious shift in thinking when watching amateur baseball where the concept of "slide or avoid contact" is used in a best effort to prevent runners from injuring fielders. Taking out a shortstop with the slide might be a quintessential baseball move but it technically is usually illegal by most rule sets. That doesn't mean all collisions on the basepath are unavoidable and/or illegal but before we look at what happens accidentally, let's first look at what the rules have to say about a runner as he slides into a base, regardless of his motivation.

In the pro game, just about anything goes regarding contact around a base **because the rules don't specifically address slides. A runner's actions, by default, are evaluated under the more general "interference" language.** As we know, the key words there are "hindering" and "altering" the play but since the runner has the right to the base, as long as he appears to be going for that base, he is considered within the rules and allowed to go in as hard as he likes. Given this creates a higher tolerance for contact, not only will you see few interference calls on a force out, I doubt you'd ever see a call if there was malicious contact, say, spikes high Ty Cobb style unless it was completely over-the-top and an obvious intent to injure. I say this because pro baseball has a way of policing itself. Hard play is respected but dirty play will draw the eye-for-an-eye treatment taking the administration of justice out of the umpire's hands. Given this, typically the only time you will see an out called for interference on a take-out slide in the pros is when the runner slides so far out of his way to make contact with the fielder that he can't reach the base. This is the tipping point where the interpretation of his motivation crosses the line from "going to" the base to "going after" the fielder, so the runner loses the benefit of the doubt. However, this concept of being able to reach the base has no specific mention in the rule books and is simply a widely accepted guideline used by umpires.

"Slide or avoid" isn't necessarily written in the rules either but the concept is typically supported by language that defines a legal slide, where actions like "sliding beyond the base" or "popping up into the fielder" are explicitly mentioned as no-nos. Whatever the verbiage, **in amateur ball, if the runner chooses to slide, he must slide directly to the base or he can slide away from the fielder**.

Where as "interference" is a judgment call and very subjective, identifying a slide as illegal is a much more objective task so policing base runners becomes easier for the umpires. This doesn't make these calls any less controversial because again, if not used to seeing it called in a pro game, there's a good chance everyone is surprised at an interference call in an amateur game, and then subsequently outraged when they realize the consequences.

The penalty for interference is that the runner will be called out as will the batter-runner and any other runners will be returned to the base they were on at the time of pitch. This is a pretty serious penalty and causes great anxiety if it appears the call was made on a technicality and not because there was actual interference. Let's look at how it should be called.

Using second base as an example, as long as the infielder is aside the base or behind it, towards left, he should be protected from potential injury because of rules prohibiting rolling or pop-up slides or any other effort to create contact or get in the way of the throw. Any contact behind or aside the base is cause for an interference call but with an emphasis on safety and preventing contact, an overzealous official might make a game changing call in a situation where the runner did nothing wrong. This can happen in a couple of scenarios.

First, the idea is that the fielder is protected behind or aside the base, not on top or in front of the base. If the fielder exposes himself to contact then you really can't blame the runner for sliding to the base and creating contact but in the instant the play demands a call, the umpire may call it interference with so much emphasis on safety.

Secondly, yes, safety is important, we got that, but was there interference? Sometimes there can be incidental contact, that technically happens in the protected area aside or behind the base, but it is after the release of the throw, so in terms of the baseball action, the slide did not cause interference, nor was it a "dirty" play. Calling an automatic double play on this technicality when there was no interference and no malicious intent on the part of the runner yields a steep penalty that serves the letter of the rule and not the spirit.

Certainly amateur players should be coached to play hard but always remember to simply slide directly to the base. If they do so and don't go beyond the base, they in theory should never risk an interference call. If there is contact, the coach should note where it is. If it is before or above the base, the runner should not be blamed and if it is not flagrant and after the release of the throw, then it can be argued there was no real interference.

Another often confusing scenario on the play at second base is when the runner doesn't slide. You will often hear a coach yell "hey, he has to slide" but in fact, **no runner ever "has to slide" according to the rules**, but he may not interfere. This typically happens when the double play is turned so quickly, the runner from first is too far from the base where a slide would serve any purpose. This is also where the principal of "slide or avoid contact" should be employed…either slide or get out of the way. The trick here is that if the runner is in line with the throw, but still 10-15 feet away, can you say he interfered by not sliding? The answer is generally, "no." The defense has to assume some level of responsibility for completing the play and if the runner is that far away, it seems reasonable an adept baseball player can make the proper adjustment. Begging for an interference call on this play is another example of looking for a freebie based on a technicality when the baseball play should take precedence over the letter of the rules. If on the other hand the runner goes all the way to the base and does not slide, then he indeed risks running right into the fielder and if this happens and causes any hitch in the middle infielders throw, then interference should indeed be called.

The difficulty of making these calls or non-calls is that they happen very quickly. Most amateur baseball games have two umpires, a plate guy and a base guy. On a double play ball, the base guy has to potentially make two close calls, one at second and one at first while also evaluating the runner's slide for illegal contact. This is a lot to watch, even for a professional umpire. What most fans don't realize is that while the base umpire can make an interference call on a play that is right in front of him, the plate umpire can just as easily make this call from a distance. In fact, if there are no runners on second or third, you should notice the plate guy initially running towards the mound on a typical double play turn at second base so he can get a good look at it. Since the base guy indeed has his hands full and must turn his attention towards first, the plate guy's job is to watch the slide and look for interference once the base umpire turns his attention towards first. So, the three keys to arguing interference at second base are A) where was the contact made, B) was there actual interference or was it after the release and C) which umpire made the call. Again, the spirit of the rule is to protect players from injury but it should also be true to the idea of interference as well. In my opinion, the call should be made only when the slide was illegal (not to the base or not beyond it) and it hindered the fielder. Precluding malicious contact, if you don't have both of these, then it is a severe call if based only on technicality.

Accidents Will Happen

We know that even when the rules of the road are closely followed, accidents happen and it's no different with base runners. Let me tell you about a game changing play that happened in a high school playoff game I worked in 2012 (3). The home team was trailing 1-0 in the bottom of the 7th (last inning) and had runners on second and third with one out when the batter hit a fly ball to center field, just deep enough for a tag up attempt from third. The same scenario played out in the bottom of the sixth and the runner was thrown out so it was doubly exciting to see the play unfolding again as an out this time would end the game.

As the runner bore down on home plate, he launched himself with a head first slide but the throw from center was a few feet up the third base line, drawing the catcher into the line of the slide. All three moving objects arrived at the same time, the ball, the runner and the catcher – the runner's dive brought him right into the catcher's chest and the ball was absorbed by the dust cloud that ensued. It was clear the runner had not reached the plate but as the dust settled I could see the ball was on the ground. Both players were a little stunned but realized there was still some baseball to be played, so as the catcher rolled around to pick up the ball, the runner was reaching over him to find the plate.

Regardless of how it turned out, you could argue the runner interfered with the catcher's effort to catch the ball or you could say the catcher obstructed the runner, blocking him without the ball as these are both violations of the letter of the rules. Which one is it? Well, if we go back to our car accident analogy, in some states, the guy whose insurance company pays is going to be the guy whose fault it was, as determined by the police report. In baseball, the arbiter is the umpire and the first thing he has to ask when an "accident" happens, is "Whose fault was it?" The way to determine that is to ask "Who did something wrong?"

In this case the runner slid directly to the plate and the catcher took a step up the line to field the ball so you can't really say anybody did anything wrong; the contact has to be looked at as simply incidental. Had the runner lowered his shoulder and crashed into the catcher or had the catcher somehow blocked the entire plate without the ball, there would be rules violations. (By the way, "malicious contact" always trumps baseball rule violations.) They both did what they were supposed to do, so as far as I was concerned, I had nothin' and it was just a matter of who would win the scramble at the plate…it turned out the catcher picked up the ball and tagged the runner a second after he rolled over to touch the plate…tie game, home crowd erupts! The home team eventually won the game in extra innings on a walk-off home run so it was a game I'll never forget.

Touch Them All – Please

I've discussed all the ways a runner can get himself out in his journey around the bases and I've left the most irresponsible one for last, missing a base. It's a pretty simple concept to score a run in baseball, just **touch all the bases and in order**. I'll talk about appeals in the next section because the burden of proof for these outs is on the defense but what I want to go over here is the responsibility of the runner. I'm always amazed when a runner fails to notice the big white square pillow laying in the middle of a swath of brown dirt but when it does happen, it's very possible it's not gross negligence but because of a baseball play that takes him out of his stride; either feet got tangled up on a wide throw or there was a slide into a base and a wild throw causing the runner to quickly get up and continue his journey without ever tagging the base. Another time you might see this happen is while legally running the bases backwards, retreating in haste because of a great catch, the runner is usually so surprised to find himself so far from where he needs to be that he doesn't retouch the base he just passed while in panic mode. **The rules are clear on this, the runner must touch each base, no matter which direction he is running.** If a base is missed on the first fly-by, touching it on the way back **will clear his earlier error as the rules say what matters is what happens on "the last time by."**

Runners must also remember that when bases are awarded when the ball leaves play, **the runner is awarded only the right to advance so he must complete the formality of touching the bases properly.** This seems obvious but let me give you a situation that might trip up a runner. Let's say a runner from first is off with the pitch in an attempt to steal and the batter hits a liner to third; the runner will be dead going back to first but let's also say the throw goes out of play behind first base. The runner will be awarded two bases bringing him to third but before he touches second and goes to third, he still has to go back and retouch first to legally tag up, even though the ball is dead. **The rules allow a runner to retouch a base after the ball is dead but only the last base acquired**. If the runner was beyond second and didn't retreat when the throw went out of play, he would lose the right to retouch first and would be subject to an out upon appeal. In fact even if he physically goes back and touches first, it wouldn't count so he might just be better off hoping that the defensive team did not notice this gaff. An out called upon appeal can turn the game upside down if it causes runs to be pulled off the board and figuring that out can be confusing.

Since the burden to make a proper appeal is on the defense, we'll cover how that works in the next section.

Final Thing About Interference, Reggie's Hip

One final note about interference: it's **an illegal act not limited to the runners, but anyone associated with the offensive team** and it doesn't have to be an act against the defense. The most common example is when a third base coach **physically assists** a runner who blasts through a stop sign and the coach reaches out to grab him; the penalty is that **the runner will be called out after the play has ended.** This is another example of a "delayed dead ball" like when the batter interferes with a catcher's throw or when the catcher interferes with the hitter's swing, the play will be allowed to finish before the call is made. Speaking of the third base coach, it is also possible he could interfere with a third baseman by not vacating the area on a pop-up and this responsibility extends to everyone in the dugout for the offensive team as well. Also, interference is not limited to physical acts but **any act that hinders a fielder's effort** so on the pop-up, if someone from offensive team's bench calls out "I got it!" to confuse the defense and it was deemed to have affected the fielder, the batter could be called out for the **verbal interference** if the ball drops uncaught.

Most of the emphasis on interference focuses on the fielders and their initial efforts to make a play on a batted ball but we can't forget about a thrown ball and this could involve the base coaches as well as the runners or other players on the field, like an on deck hitter coaching at home plate. I briefly touched on this earlier when describing a double play ball where the runner doesn't slide but that's more of an effort to disrupt the turn than the throw itself. Since most runners who are hit with throws are hit on the back, it has to be viewed as incidental since the throw is chasing them to a base. It should be pretty difficult to intentionally interfere with a throw and not have it appear obvious to everyone in the park but this is exactly what happened in the 1978 World Series in one of the crazier and more disputed plays in playoff history:

- The culprit: Reginald Martinez Jackson.
- The setting: Yankee Stadium, game four of the World Series.
- The situation: runners on 1st and 2nd and one out.
- The action: line drive to short.

With the Dodgers ahead in the game 3-0 and threatening to take a commanding 3-1 lead in games, the Yankees rallied in the bottom of the 6th to break the ice against Dodger starter Tommy John. Reggie Jackson singled home Roy White to make it 3-1 and Lou Piniella came up with Jackson on first and Thurman Munson on second. Piniella hit a line drive to short, a little to his left but a very catchable ball for Dodger shortstop Bill Russell. Both runners retreated to their respective bases to avoid being doubled off but alas, Russell muffed the ball. Seeing the ball on the ground, Munson alertly bolted for third avoiding a tag but Russell stepped on second for the force out and fired to first for an easy double play and the apparent third out.

Jackson, now a retired runner, was only a few feet off first following Russell's non-catch and found himself in the line of the throw to first baseman Steve Garvey; frozen for a moment, he ever so slightly stuck out his hip to deflect the throw down the right field line allowing Munson to come around and score. Legendary Dodger skipper Tommy Lasorda was livid at the non call and put up a heroic argument going so far as to reenact Reggie's nonchalant hands on hip dance move that deflected the ball; the replay clearly caught Reggie leaning into the throw. The crew, a mix of umpires from both leagues, didn't budge and Piniella was not called out because of Reggie's actions, Munson's run stayed on the board and the stage was set

146

for the Yankees comeback and 10th inning walk off hit by none other than Reggie Jackson himself.

While the non-call seemingly turned the momentum irrevocably towards the Bronx Bombers in the game and series, the real unsung star of the tale is the non-catch by Russell. While this is a discussion more suited for the section of the book on defense, I have to point it out here. Russell clearly muffed the ball with the intention of turning an easy double play but the baseball gods beseeched Jackson to turn this around on the Dodgers. The rules prevent a player from intentionally dropping the ball and offer the runners the same protection as the Infield Fly Rule so as soon as a ball is intentionally dropped, **time is called, the batter is called out and the runners are put back on their bases.** The ensuing confusion and mayhem on the bases in the Dodger-Yankee game is exactly what the rule attempts to avoid and once again, prohibits players from doing the opposite of what they are supposed to do, in this case, catch the ball. To show a little bit of fairness to the second base umpire, this is a judgment call but if you look at the video, I think you'll agree Russell intentionally and just so matter-of-factly dropped the ball going straight to his left towards second base. This play has gone down in history as a devious example of a retired runner interfering and getting away with it but it's more of a tale of a fielder breaking the rules and not-getting away with it, but for all the wrong reasons.

No Lollygagging, Timing is everything

One last thing about circling the bases, players should be taught to hustle to the plate and score even when they know there will be no play on them because there might be a play on another runner and then, the timing play is in effect. You've probably never noticed but anytime there is a runner on second base with two outs, the umpires will signal to each other by

147

tapping the spot on their wrist where they would wear a watch; this is to remind the plate guy that if there is a

Non-force out for the third out, he has to notice if the runner crosses the plate before the out, so the run can count. One of the simpler examples of a timing play occurs with one out and runners on second and third and the batter hits a fly ball to the outfield. If both runners tag up and the center fielder decides to throw to third, the runner advancing home might lollygag, but if the trailing runner is out at third before he crosses the plate, his run won't count. It's possible to have a timing play combined with an appeal of a missed base mixed in and everyone will be confused but I'll keep you guessing until the section on defense, when I cover appeals.

Part III Footnotes

(1) The "eephus" pitch is basically just a slow ball thrown with a high arc, not unlike slow-pitch softball, popularized by Pirates pitcher Rip Sewell in the 30s and 40s. Bill Lee retired Tony Perez twice on this pitch in game 7 but when he tried once too many, Perez crushed a 2 run homer his 3rd time up sparking the Red's comeback. I was in the park with my SRO ticket so without a seat, I spent a good portion of the game simply strolling the main aisle that runs from first to third base at Fenway Park. I was directly behind home plate for that pitch and got a look at both the arced pitch and moon shot over the wall from less than 90 feet away.

(2) Edison Rosanda Armbrister, born July 4, 1948 in Nassau, Bahamas. Played part of 5 seasons for Reds as a reserve outfielder, (1973-1977), a career .245 hitter with 302 at-bats.

(3) In Encinitas, California between host team San Dieguito Academy (coached by 1993 AL Cy Young winner Jack McDowell) and Santana HS.

The Rules Abide!

Part IV – The Defense

After tracking batters and runners around the diamond, it's finally time to talk about the defense and the rules that affect them most. We've already explored the mysterious world of the pitcher in the balk discussion and explored action around the plate with his battery mate, the catcher, so that leaves us with a more general discussion about the simple acts of catching and throwing the ball that apply to all fielders. You'll find fewer specific rule references in this section but with guidelines for remembering base awards, an in depth discussion about obstruction and some deep cuts exploring appeals and other specific and interesting situations, I still think there's lots of meat on the bone when talking about defense, I mean, have you ever heard of the fourth out?

Glove is All Around!

There are two very unique elements of baseball that the other major sports lack, there is no clock and in baseball, the defense holds the ball...ideally! This creates an ever present tension to the game because the defense is never taken off the hook by a clock ticking down and as long as there is still at least one out to go, the offense still has hope, however slim.

The game may end on a hit, the "walk-off", which is always exciting but more often than not, hope is snuffed out as the ball settles into a glove which is squeezed tightly. It might only be a routine play, like when closer Keith Foulke tossed the ball to Doug Mientkiewicz to capture the 2004 World Series for the Red Sox, but a simple catch removes all doubt, and in this case, released 86 years of angst for Boston fans.

And then there are the great catches. Anyone over forty probably immediately thinks about the iconic image of the most famous catch ever, Willie Mays over the shoulder grab in game one of the 1954 World Series. With the game on the line in the late innings, the Indians Vic Wertz launched a bomb deep to center field and Mays, running with his back to the plate in the enormous confines of the old Polo Grounds in New York, caught the ball over his left shoulder about 425 feet from the plate and spun to double Larry Doby off second. This play was on the big stage of the World Series in a tight spot in a tight game and could only have happened on that field as the ball would have been a home run in any other stadium. A web-gem that went viral, before there was such a thing, it will forever remain an iconic catch and highlight from the early days of television and the golden age of baseball.

We could go on and on about great catches but in all likelihood the most memorable catch you ever saw probably happened in an amateur baseball game on a dusty field, somewhere off the beaten path a long time ago, maybe a catch that clinched a local championship. Witnessed by few, it provided no less an indelible image in your mind than May's catch and reminds us that baseball is great wherever you find it. The game, bigger than all of us but still very personal, proves a small makeshift church is no less a sanctuary than St. Patrick's cathedral. The key to all baseball catches is that the player demonstrates control and possession of the ball, not unlike how you hold on to those memories!

The Atomic Structure of a Catch

However straightforward the definition of a catch is, **getting secure possession of the ball in the hand or glove**, or however routine a play is, there are three components to legally catching the baseball that need to be understood in order to evaluate a play: securing the ball, holding it until the continued action of the play is complete and lastly, making a movement to begin the next play.

One of the best plays I ever made as a third baseman in the adult leagues came on a throw from the outfield to nail a hitter digging for a triple. The relay from left-center field caught me with one of those in-between hops, not a short one that bounces right in the mitt and not a long one which gives you a fighting chance to actually react to the bounce of the ball, but the middle one where you hold your glove open in a best-guess position and you hope you don't take one in the crotch! In one swift movement I snatched at the ball and dropped the glove on the runner's feet and got the exciting out call to end the inning on a beautiful June Sunday afternoon at lovely Amory Field in Brookline, Massachusetts.

I know what you are thinking, "okay, big deal, you handled a tricky throw, so what?"...and I agree, no, the best part of the play was that I didn't catch that tricky hop but got lucky as the ball wedged perfectly under my left armpit, the other crotch! In a moment of clarity and pure improvisation, I simply squeezed my left arm, chicken dance style to keep control, made the tag and headed for our bench a few feet away on the third base side...now you see it, now you don't!

That was a good one and served to remind us that we should always keep our eye on the ball in baseball because a catch and tag is legal only **when the fielder holds the ball securely in the hand or glove and uses that hand or glove to make the tag**. With two God-given hands, presumably complete with opposable thumbs, and a tool designed specifically to enhance the ability to catch and hold a baseball, a fielder should have everything he needs to get the job done and the rules agree. **The ball shall not be trapped against the body** (my trick) **or other object like the ground or a fence and not make use of any detached equipment** like a hat or catcher's mask. Sure the fielder can juggle the ball and it could even go from one fielder to another but the ball has to eventually be held securely only in the glove or hand.

This discussion makes me think of two very memorable plays in the majors, both timeless web gems. The first was San Francisco outfielder Kevin Mitchell's barehanded catch in 1989 and the second is ironically, a non-catch, the fly ball that hit Jose Canseco in the head in 1993. Mitchell, running hard towards the left-field foul line, overran Ozzie Smith's fly ball in foul ground and reached up and behind his head with his right hand to make a one-of-a-kind bare-handed catch, demonstrating you don't need no stinkin' glove to make a catch, although it's a very good idea to use it if you can, Jose. At the other end of the spectrum you have Canseco, playing outfield for Texas at the time, drifting back on the warning track to snare a long fly by the Indian's Carlos Martinez, but as he leapt, missed the ball, got clunked on the head and the ball disappeared over the fence on the bounce...for a home run. Mitchell's catch was just an oddity but Canseco's blooper proves anything can happen and is a little more thought provoking. Let's have Jose help us look at other impossibly possible scenarios and how they are resolved with respect to the rules:

- Ball clunks Canseco in fair ground and bounces over fence in foul ground - ground rule double.
- Ball clunks Canseco and hits foul pole above fence line - home run.
- Ball clunks Canseco and is then secured on the fly by second baseman – catch.
- Ball clunks Canseco and is caught by centerfielder in his hat – not a catch.
- Ball clunks Canseco, bounces off center fielder and is caught by Canseco – catch.
- Ball clunks Canseco, hits wall and is caught - not a catch.
- Ball clunks Canseco, hits umpire and is caught - not a catch.
- Ball clunks Canseco and comes down in his back pocket – not a catch.
- Ball clunks Canseco, knocks him out cold, lands on his belly - not a catch as the ball is not held securely in hand or glove, that is until Canseco wakes up or another fielder grabs the ball.
- Canseco falls over outfield rail, lands in seats, ball clunks him on head and is caught – home run.

Okay, these are crazy examples, and I could provide more, but they serve to illustrate the rules and allow me to write "ball clunks Canseco" over and over which I can't get enough of. Deflections are okay as long **as the ball doesn't hit the ground, a fence or any other object ("unnatural to the ground") other than the defensive player** and **a ball that ricochets off a runner or umpire counts as hitting the ground too.** I mentioned this earlier but one serious lesson from this for base runners involves tag ups: as soon as the ball clunks Canseco's head (bonus reference), runners are allowed to legally leave their base as they do not have to wait until the play is complete, only that the ball clunks Canseco's head (double bonus reference).

Another very serious lesson about catches has to do with being in-play or out, as illustrated in that last clunks-Canseco example. Obviously if the fielder leaves the playing field completely, he is considered out of play so in the example, even though he caught the ball, it is a home run.

If the same scenario played out on a foul ball, it would not be a catch, just a foul ball.

A more likely scenario is a player who makes a great catch but falls over a wall. **As long as any part of the fielder is still "in-play" when he secures the ball, it is a legal catch. In amateur games, where lines on the ground more often determine the playing field than a wall, as long as the player has one toe still in play, a catch is legal.** When a player dives over a short fence, as long as it appears he is not completely over the fence when he makes the catch, it is also good. Around the dugouts, the same principal holds true and in fact, **it's legal for a player to be physically assisted so he doesn't fall into the dugout while making a catch.**

What is really important for players to be aware of, however, is that **after they make a catch and leave play, the ball becomes dead and all runners are entitled to one extra base.** In the pros there is a distinction made between "stepping" completely in dead-ball territory and "falling" into dead-ball territory and the **ball is only dead if**

the player "falls" . In theory, if a player makes a catch with one foot on the top step of the dugout and then goes into the dugout and stays on his feet, it is a good catch and the play is allowed to continue. If that same player falls down in the dugout after legally making the catch, the play is dead and all runners are awarded one base. If the ball clunks Canseco on the head and then he catches it, but then falls over the rail in the outfield, it would be an out and all runners, who still need to tag up of course, would be awarded one base.

You might have also heard of a ground rule known as "catch and carry" and this is something used mostly in amateur games as an override to the dead-ball rule. "Catch and carry" means as long as the catch is legal the player may carry the ball over a line marking dead-ball territory and still legally make a throw from that spot. This is used on fields that have a lot of foul ground and no fences so it allows for a boundary that determines if batted balls are in play but makes those boundaries moot once a fielder has made a legal catch. Without a three dimensional boundary like a fence to get in the way, there is no reason the play should be killed; if the runners are to get an extra base, they need to tag up on their own.

An Object in Motion Stays in Motion!

The second component of a catch is the continued action that takes place between the fielder first making contact with the ball and the third step, the voluntary action to do something else, like make a throw or scratch an itch. There might not be any continued action on a routine play but any effort that has a degree of difficulty more than a five out of ten probably has the fielder covering a lot of ground and where there is motion, there is inertia or momentum, which is a force that must play itself out until acted upon by another force, if I may be so semi-scientific. The "other force" is going to be the player himself or another object like a fence or the ground so when you have the makings of a great play, it can't be ruled a catch until the continued action is complete or in other words, the player has to catch himself first before his catch of the ball is deemed complete. If the ball comes out of the glove as the fielder rolls over following a dive or after two or three steps following a long running "catch", it should not be declared a catch if you can't say the release of the ball was voluntary and you can't very well say the fielder's intent was to put the ball on the ground either. This doesn't mean the player has to come to a complete stop, only that he regains his composure so he may make the next move.

I once saw a third baseman dive directly toward the batter to snatch a hot line drive but instead of getting his glove under the ball, he caught it with the palm of his hand facing home plate. He had the ball in his glove but his dive left him in an awkward position lying on his stomach, arms extended, in a sky-diver's position, like he just jumped out of a plane. Not knowing how to make the next move he tried to hold still for a second or two to demonstrate control but then, like a boat capsizing, he rolled belly-up, the ball came loose and the umpires, correctly and emphatically ruled "no catch." The player and manager argued he clearly had control of the ball long enough but his roll was the continued action of the initial catch and this trumps the time argument. This is a good place to point out that **the rule book does not specify how long the fielder must hold the ball, only long enough to prove that he has complete control of the ball,** but again, if he is not in control of himself, you can't assume he is in control of the ball.

The key language here are the words "**voluntary and intentional**" as they relate to why the ball came loose. Let's compare a diving fielder's effort to an actual dive into a swimming pool. Is the dive complete when the diver touches the water? Not exactly, you wouldn't say the diver is making a next move until he begins his ascent and swim to the edge of the pool and it's the same thing with a diving catch of the baseball, the play isn't over until he voluntarily and intentionally makes a move to make another baseball play, or you could say, comes up for air!

"Go Ahead, Make My Day" – The Next Move

Since the transitional phase of a catch, the continued action, doesn't always happen, the trickiest plays to judge are those where the player goes directly from making contact with the ball and making the next play which happens in a fraction of a second. While there is for the most part no distinction between catching a batted ball versus a thrown ball, lets quickly look at the classic call of "on the transfer", when middle infielders lose handle of the ball when attempting to turn a double play. What typically happens is that as the fielder takes the ball out of his glove, he loses grip and the ball comes out in a manner that is clearly not related to the trajectory of the initial throw or hit. Let's look at a second baseman taking a throw from the shortstop - the throw comes from the hole let's say but when he loses control taking it out of his glove, it usually winds up going backwards, behind second base towards center or left-center, because that is the direction his hand was going as he took the ball out of his glove in an attempt to cock his arm, which is completely different than the direction of the throw. This change of direction is usually what indicates the ball came loose on the transfer. If it comes out straight to the ground or looks like a simple bounce out of the glove, then it should be clear that it is not a catch at all. Going back to the language of "voluntary and intentional", we can see that the ball came out of the glove after an intentional move, so the out at second stands based on a nanosecond of possession.

There doesn't necessarily have to be a throw following the play however, a catch for the third out for example. Sometimes a fielder will drop the ball as he brings his glove from an outstretched position required to make the catch close to his body in a position that is comfortable for the jog to the dugout and this would be considered a catch because that move to recoil from the extension is indeed voluntary and intentional and not simply inertia. I can give all sorts of examples but really the key are those words…I'll repeat them one more time, **"voluntary and intentional."** The next time you are watching a baseball game, see what happens the moment after the catch with respect to those words and it will become easy for you to recognize when a catch is complete. You've probably seen umpires wait to see that the ball is cleanly held on a sliding out before making an out call but you won't notice an umpire making a delayed call on a routine out. Sure, it's obvious to everyone in the park the batter was out by 10 feet but he might wait until he sees the first baseman transfer that ball to his throwing hand or make some other voluntary move before signaling.

As I said a moment ago there is one slight variation for determining a catch for a throw or a batted ball and that has to do with the ground. Obviously a batted ball that hits the ground first cannot be called for an out. We've all seen disputed short-hop catches and since that is simply a judgment call, there is not much debate about the rules. I will say that sharp eyes will notice that miniscule hop but it takes an even sharper eye to notice when a diving fielder gets his glove underneath the ball and what looks like a short hop off the grass to most observers is indeed a catch because the ball never hit the ground…but I digress. Yes, a batted ball that touches the ground cannot be caught for an out but a thrown ball is a different story and it involves the baseball icon, the "snow cone", that ball that is barely held in the glove while 2/3rds of the orb extends above the pocket, lookin' like a snow cone (1). A first baseman, for example, who is catching a throw for a force out could be in control of the ball, via the snow cone, but have the ball touch the ground simultaneously. Another example is a fielder who drops the initial throw but then squeezes the ball on the ground with his bare hands. Whereas this would not be deemed a catch on a batted ball, it would indeed count as control of a thrown ball because it is held securely in the hand or glove.

And one final, final, thing about catches specific to one particular defensive player, the catcher and his good buddy, the foul-tip. I don't think I need to explain the concept of the foul-tip but it is something you should know is not as automatic as you think. The vast majority of the time the ball is caught crisply and play continues as though the ball was never touched, which is the whole point of the darned thing. Sometimes, however, the ball changes direction after the slightest contact with the bat and rattles around in the catchers lap, and as long as it doesn't touch the ground is usually still called a foul tip and possible third strike but here is what the rules say. **A foul tip is a ball that goes directly to the catcher's hands and is caught. If it hits the mitt first and rattles around and is subsequently secured also in the catcher's hands, it is treated as a catch and the ball is live and in play, just as though it was a swinging strike. However, if it hits the catcher any place other than the hands - the gut, the chest protector or thighs, anywhere - and is subsequently caught in the hands, it is not a legal foul tip and should be called foul and a dead-ball.** Just in case you were wondering!

Block, Tripp & Obstruction...

In its simplest form, **obstruction is the act of a fielder who impedes the progress of any runner while not in possession of the ball and not in the act of fielding the ball.** This is a pretty simple concept - without the ball being involved, it's pretty obvious when a fielder blocks a runner. A classic example is a batter digging for extra bases who runs into the first baseman while rounding the base. There doesn't have to be contact, just like with interference, as long as the act causes the runner to alter his gate or path. This is not something you will see often in the pro game as it's just not a mistake professionals make and with four umpires typically on the field, someone is always watching.

You won't see it called very often in amateur baseball either. It's not because it doesn't happen, but because there are fewer umpires with higher priorities than finding obstructions away from the ball. Most amateur games have only one or two umpires and their heads are on a swivel watching the ball and the base touches so runners often become invisible to umpires when they are between bases. If an obstruction is noticed away from the ball, the umpire will wait until the play is finished before calling time and **placing the runner on the base he feels he would have reached had there not been obstruction, another case of a delayed dead-ball.** It's a little different when obstruction occurs near the ball, like in a sloppy run down play with too many throws when a fielder doesn't get out of the way and blocks the runner who quickly reverses direction after a throw.

There are two nuances to obstruction on these plays: one is that that the umpires will call time out immediately, because the runner is trapped and the other is that he must be moved along at least one base forward, not necessarily the base he was racing towards. Let's say the runner is caught between third and home and as he makes a break back to third and slides, he is blocked from the bag and then tagged. The defense will argue that he should be placed on third, since that's where he was headed, but because he already touched and passed third, the award has to be that he goes to the next base, home plate, and scores. Keeping him at third would mean there is effectively no penalty to the obstruction since he already reached that base.

While contact that impedes a runner away from the ball is textbook obstruction, primarily because by definition, it is away from the ball, it is much less obvious and much more controversial when considering obstruction around a base as a runner slides in ahead of the throw. The qualifier on the rule book definition is that the fielder must not have the ball nor be in the act of fielding it, but this leads me to two questions. Isn't it just enough to say, obstruction is "an act of a fielder who impedes the progress of any runner"? Second, where in the rule book does it say you can ever block a base? It doesn't, as it is only implied by the qualifiers "not in possession of the ball or in the act of fielding it." This is another way of saying that if you have possession of the ball or you're in the act of fielding the ball, then you can prevent the runner access to the base and this is where I have a bone to pick with the rule book. Why should a defensive player ever be allowed to block a base? Sure, you can argue the big boy game is played all-out and that contact is part of the game but in the amateur game, in my experience, most injuries occur because of contact at a base and I'm not sure this contact is essential to the game. Let me put it another way, if a fielder stuck his foot out to trip a runner, wouldn't every one agree that is an obvious example of obstruction? So then, how in the name of Bruno Block or Brandon Tripp did it become a good play to stick your foot in front of the base to prevent the runner access and then tag him once you catch the ball? (2) In my opinion, this is no different from an obvious obstruction, except that the trip occurs in the last inch before the base rather than ten or twenty feet from it.

The benefit of the doubt the fielder generally gets, when the ball is in the neighborhood, leads to more contact because fielders know they have this leeway. They tend to do what comes naturally, drop a leg in front of a base or put their whole body in between the runner and the base when making a tag. When not making a tag, usually at first base, you will often see the first baseman step right in front of a runner to chase a wide throw. Since the burden of avoiding collisions in amateur ball is with the runner, he will often slow down or run wide further increasing his chance of being put out. Unfortunately, the only way to draw the obstruction call is to create contact so the way I see it, there's a disconnect between what the rule is trying to prevent and how it is written and enforced, that is, it's not called very much. I understand that sometimes contact is incidental and unavoidable and I am not trying to promote a culture of fear about injuries; I'm just sharing my observations about how the game is played with respect to the rules and in

162

this case, just thinking out loud and wondering how radical would it be to say that unless reaching with a glove or hand, the burden for avoiding contact should fall on the fielder. Couple this with proper slide rules already in place in amateur ball and you would have a game played and officiated more in line with the spirit of the obstruction rule. Certainly at the high school level I would say this non-call of obstruction is one of the most argued plays in the game and that is a direct result of the rule that implies that while in the act of receiving the ball, the fielder can block the base.

Tricks and Small Travesties

Just as there are non-physical ways for someone on the offense to interfere with the defense, verbally for instance, there are other ways to obstruct the offense as well, other than the obvious. Some amateur rule books go further than the standard definition of what constitutes obstruction and this can include verbal obstruction or other tricks, like faking a tag. In high school, where safety is always important, a player who fakes a tag and causes a runner to slide unnecessarily is cause for an obstruction call while it might be considered a slick play at the pro level. In fact, all kinds of decoys and trick plays could be considered obstruction because the fielder, without the ball, does something to impede the runner, but these are allowed, unless specifically mentioned like the fake tag, as long as they don't make a travesty of the game. Even at the high school level you will see things like the hidden ball trick that might be considered "bush league" but are none the less allowed because there isn't a rule that says you can't do it.

Also, there is a certain burden of responsibility placed upon players to know the situation in the game so if they are duped, the rules are not going to bail them out. If, for example, there was an act by the defense to trick the runner into thinking there were three outs when there were only two, the runner can't blame anyone but himself for knowing how many outs there are, nor should he. In fact, even if the umpire screwed up and told him the wrong number of outs, it was still his initial responsibility to know; even though the umpire was wrong, it doesn't get him off the hook; two wrongs still don't make a right! Just to give you an idea of the kind of tricks I'm talking about, let me tell you about one I saw in a freshman high school game here in southern California. With a runner on second base, the pitcher spun and motioned a throw to second. The runner dove back but both the shortstop and second baseman ran into short centerfield as though it were an overthrow. The center fielder also turned his back and ran towards right center chasing down that crazy throw. The trap was set and the runner bit, it had to be a wild throw so he took off for third and fell victim to a highly orchestrated act by a well rehearsed troupe and was thrown out easily by the pitcher who had the ball all along. So, the question is, does this make a travesty of the game or is it smart baseball? It's not clear the rules offer a definitive answer.

And speaking of travesties in the game of baseball, although mentioned in the rule book in the section on running the bases backwards, it's not something that manifests itself in the context of game situations often, if at all, but is fodder for discussion on a grander scale.

Some could say the DH is a travesty of the game (not me); some could argue steroids made a travesty of the game. We used to think cookie-cutter stadiums with artificial turf made a travesty of the game and thankfully, the powers that be came around on that one. These are larger issues you can liken to societal changes, like wearing seatbelts and smoking, that over time realize a significant shift in public thinking resulting in progress, which can be debated all day long and very seriously at that. Since I'm exploring the rules, I want to look at game specifics and if there is one case for making a travesty of the game, that has to be looked at with humor not scrutiny, we have to go back and look at a caper pulled off by the legendary team owner, Bill Veeck Jr., in 1951.

Veeck (1914-1986), the son and namesake of the Chicago Cubs president from 1919-1933, grew up around the game at Wrigley Field and developed into a great showman and forward thinker who eventually owned three major league teams at various times: The Cleveland Indians, The St. Louis Browns and The Chicago White Sox.

A master at rankling traditional sensibilities, the controversial owner's legacy includes some serious accomplishments, like signing the American League's first Afro-American player, Larry Doby, and testifying in favor of free agency, and against his fellow owners in the 70s, but he is more famously known for an array of creative and light hearted publicity stunts over the decades (3).

One of his most famous promotions came in his first year of ownership of the Browns. On August 19th, 1951 he secretly signed little person Eddie Gaedel to a one day contract. Gaedel, a professional performer, stood 3 feet 7 inches tall and was hired to pop out of a cake between games of a doubleheader to promote Falstaff beer. As far as cake-popping and beer promotion goes, I imagine a Marilyn Monroe look-a-like might have been a better choice as far as the Falstaff people were concerned but Veeck had bigger plans that day, no pun intended.

In the bottom of the first inning of game two, shortly after popping out of the cake, Gaedel popped out of the dugout, this time with a bat over his shoulder in a new role, that of pinch hitter and made the long walk to the plate wearing uniform number 1/8th and elf like shoes. The umpire played the perfect foil and called Browns' manager Zach Taylor out to challenge the legality of Eddie's presence but Veeck was one small step ahead, as usual. Having filed Gaedel's contract with the league office on Friday afternoon, Veeck knew nobody would look at it until Monday so by default and common custom, the little guy would be good for the Sunday double header versus Detroit. Handed the contract by the manager, the umpire had no choice but to let the show go on so with the biggest of hearts and smallest of strike zones, Gaedel stepped in the box and promptly drew a walk on four pitches to the pleasure of the home crowd. Replaced by a pinch runner as soon as he reached first, after twice stopping for bows, Gaedel received a standing ovation from the 18,000 plus fans, including the Falstaff reps, and the rest is history. First thing the following Monday, the league voided the contract, of course, saying Veeck was making a mockery of the game and the feisty owner shot back threatening to request a ruling on whether or not Yankee shortstop Phil Rizzuto, at 5 feet 6 inches, was a short ball player or tall midget. Travesty is surely in the eye of the beholder and as you can imagine, the league immediately changed their policy about rubber stamping contracts after the Gaedel deal.

It's a Judgment Call

Before we talk about the larger issue of fixed base running awards, let's review a couple of **other infractions where the awards, like obstruction, are based on umpire judgment, spectator interference and defensive malicious contact**.

The key to determining spectator interference is to know who owns what turf. There are physical boundaries like walls and fences that outline the playing field but baseball is an intimate game and in pro-baseball there are plenty of opportunities for the players and fans to come face-to-face, down in the expensive seats, where only an imaginary line separate the two. **When a fielder is reaching into the stands and breaking this invisible plane,** a la the infamous situation at Wrigley field in the 2003 playoffs (4) **the ball is considered in the fan's turf so the players reach in at their own risk.**

If a fan reaches over the fence and breaks the plane coming from the other side, he has reached onto the players' turf and any contact with the ball or

distraction to the fielder should be considered interference. This typically happens on a ball hit down the line and headed for the corners when a fan will reach over, catch the souvenir and sit down quickly thinking nobody saw him. The ball is dead of course and the runners will be placed where the umpires deem appropriate, usually two bases since it's like a ground rule double, and the fan will be sent home! Those are simple cases because the fan reached over before the player was in the area. Where it gets dicey, like the Bartman incident, which clearly wasn't interference, is when the players and fans fight for the same space, as it was the night of October 9, 1996 in game 1 of the ALCS, a playoff game between the Yankees and Orioles that produced, arguably, the most famous interference controversy in history.

With the Yankees trailing 4-3 in the bottom of the 8th inning, Derek Jeter launched a fly towards the legendary short porch in right field at old Yankee Stadium. Just as right fielder Tony Tarasco backed up and settled under it, soon to be Yankee legend, Jeffrey Maier, an 11 year old fan sitting in the first row, reached over the wall and snatched the ball with his glove. Umpire Richie Garcia ruled it a home run, tying the game at 4, although the replay clearly showed this was interference because Maier reached down to catch the ball which wouldn't have left the yard otherwise. The problem, other than the blown call itself, was that this was in the days before instant replay was used to review such plays and since it was a judgment call by the umpire, there was no recourse for Orioles' manager Davey Johnson. The Yankees went on to win the game in 11 innings, the championship series, and the World Series but who knows what would have happened had they lost that first game. Had Garcia ruled interference he could have called it an out or if he felt the ball would not be caught, awarded Jeter the appropriate bases, and probably put him on second.

Malicious contact is something you will rarely see in the pros outside of a hit batter's charge to the mound, which is cause for ejection, because, as we discussed earlier, runners are allowed to bowl over a catcher and the game tends to police itself regarding cheap shots. In amateur ball, where tempers or composure might be short, if a player is observed do anything considered malicious, sliding with the intent to injure, intentionally throwing at a batter, lowering a shoulder to run over a catcher, **time out will be called immediately, the offender will be called out and no other runner will be allowed to advance beyond the last base touched prior to the malicious contact.**

Base Awards & Penalties

As we just covered, some awards are based on umpire judgment but most other base awards are very specific and fixed. Baseball rule books usually contain a table of awards that can be difficult to memorize because of all the unusual ways a ball can be declared out of play or dead and by the time these rarities occur, it's hard to recall the proper ruling.

I'm going to take a different approach and try to present a table-less table, and discuss the principles behind the awards so they make sense if you logically think them through, rather than trying to remember all the weird plays by rote.

The first new idea that will help with these is to realize that most "awards" are actually "penalties", that is, they are handed out not because the offense did something good, but because the defense screwed up. With the exception of a home run over the fence or a ground rule double, pretty much everything else is a form of punishment: the pitcher balks - penalty, an outfielder throws the ball out of the stadium - penalty, pitcher hits the batter in the head -penalty...you see where this is going? Not only is it easier to think of them as penalties, but it will make even more sense once you see the rationale for the number of bases.

One, Two...

The amount of bases handed out following a dead-ball can be one, two, three or four bases. The most important piece of information when determining base awards is to know the timing of the infraction; did it happen before or after the ball was put in play? A simple question, but let me explain why the answer is so important. Yes, bases handed out for something like a bad throw is indeed a penalty, but part of that penalty takes into consideration that the batter at the very least put the ball in play and is entitled to something for that effort. By that, I mean there is usually a base awarded to accord the hitter for doing something good (hitting the ball) and then an additional base as penalty to the defense for doing something bad (throwing it away). If the batter didn't put the ball in play however, then runners, including the batter, are typically accorded only one base, for the defensive mistake, like a wild pick off throw that leaves play. This is my wordy way of saying that anything that happens on the pitch is a one base penalty: balks, wild pitches that go out of play, catcher's obstruction, batter hit by pitch, etc, but if the penalty is awarded after the ball is put in play, then you typically have a two base award/penalty. I know that is obvious for the usual plays but this simple guideline will help you understand the awards/penalties for the quirky stuff that you don't see very often. For example, a pitch that lodges in the catcher's or umpire's uniform would only be a one base award as it is no different than a pitch that goes out of bounds in the usual way, instead of going into what you normally think of as dead-ball territory, it disappeared in a uniform. If a batted ball did the same, two bases. I'll get into some complexities about how the awards are applied but this simple guideline will help you understand the number of bases on just about every infraction.

Three, Four…

I mentioned earlier that a home run is the only **4-base award if the ball goes over the fence of course but also if it hits the foul pole above the fence line or is prevented from going over the fence by a fan or detached equipment**, a thrown glove for example, regardless if the ball clunks Canseco's head or not, as long as it doesn't touch the ground first. That said, **there is only one 3-base award and that is for a batted ball not headed over the fence that is touched by detached equipment or an illegal glove or mitt (5)**. We think of a thrown glove when we hear "detached player equipment" but this includes the catcher's mask which could be used to scoop up a batted ball or a cap. If the catcher uses his mask to scoop up a bunt that's only two feet in front of the plate, well then, that is our one and only three-base award, a batted ball touched by detached player equipment. If you think of the absurdity of throwing the glove then you can understand why this penalty is so harsh and has an extra base assigned to the penalty which makes it an exception to the put-in-play test but if you remember it as the only 3-base award, it will stick.

Okay, so without a table to remember, now you know the difference between 1 and 2-base awards and you also know there is only one 3-base award and one 4-base award. Let's keep going and talk about the few exceptions. Since we're talking about the catcher and the harshness of the detached equipment bases (three), also note that if a hat or mask was used on a pitch or a throw, not a batted ball, then the award is two bases not three. Handing out two bases for doing this on a throw from another fielder is consistent with our guideline because it is after the ball is put in play but **the two base award on the loose pitch that is scooped up with the mask is an exception; everything else on the pitch yields a 1-base award, except the use of detached equipment which yields 2.**

170

Let's review the tableless table:

- 1 Base – everything on the pitch (with exception of detached player equipment)
- 2 Bases – everything after the ball is put in play
- 3 Bases – Batted ball touched by detached or illegal equipment
- 4 Bases – home run or home run interrupted

One more clarification on base running awards/penalties: when I say the ball is "put in play" you probably think I mean it is batted but let's be more precise. Let's think of "in play" as the action that happens once the physical pitch is completed and by that I mean after the ball is either hit or secured by the catcher. The ball that gets away from the catcher might create a little gray area so let's look at how we draw the line on that. Imagine the catcher is tracking down a wild ball four and before he even gets a chance to stop the ball, it is swallowed up by the dugout and becomes dead.

Well, you know by our simple rule, that since it happened on the pitch, it is only a 1-base award but the offense might argue for an additional base. You could make the case, I suppose, that once the runner reached first base or a guy already on base advanced to the next one before the ball became dead, they should be awarded an extra base for their hustle but the basic premise of the game is that the offense must earn its way around the bases, so two bases when the ball wasn't put in play amounts to a double award for one act, a pitched ball four, and this is not consistent with our rule. But let's take it one step further; let's say that as the catcher frantically slid on his knees towards the dugout he inadvertently knocked the ball out of play. What do you think should happen? In this case the runner(s) would indeed get two bases from the time of the infraction because once the catcher made a play on it, the ball transitioned from being "on the pitch" to being "in play" by my definition. If the pitch went out of play on its own, then it is a one-base penalty, but if the catcher's actions caused it to go out of play, then it is a two-base penalty. In this case, had the runner hustled to first before the ball was kicked into the dugout, he would indeed be awarded third. Notice the important distinctions in my argument:

- "In play" doesn't mean hit, only that the pitch is complete.
- "Out-of-play" is out-of-play so every dead-ball area is treated the same.
- We don't distinguish how it went out of play, dead is dead.

So with a simple understanding of the difference between "on the pitch" or "in play" and a broadened understanding of "out of play", there is no penalty we should have a hard time assessing. Let's test our theory. I don't remember the players involved, but I saw a highlight on ESPN one night of a hard grounder towards second that took a bad hop and hit the second baseman's jaw and ricocheted into his jersey. Somehow as his instincts took over to protect himself he twisted his torso and threw his head back and the ball caromed right down the front of his jersey. What's the call? Well, we know it was a batted ball in play and we know it went into dead-ball territory so it's no different than your garden variety ground rule double, batter goes to second and all other runners advance two bases. Simple right? Let's try a few more:

- Catcher's interference – batter is awarded one base because the interference happened before the ball was hit, on the pitch.
- Batted ball is caught with an illegal glove – ball is in play so two bases.
- Throw by shortstop lodges in first baseman's shirt on the hop – ball in play is thrown out of play, two bases.

So, you see, our logic is holding up but there are always exceptions and here are a couple that you'll agree make sense. A batted ball that hits an umpire or runner may be interference, but the batter is only awarded one base not two and this seems to go against our rules. Well, the umpire is a neutral party so you can't blame the defense for the interference so it's not a penalty-base on top of an award-base, it's only the one base the offense earned for hitting the ball. And the same is true for the ball that hits the runner as you can't penalize the defense for something the offense did, so that is one base as well. I realize these explanations might be longer than a detailed table but again, I'm explaining these so you can remember the common sense behind them.

What Time is it, Pitch or Throw?

The rules have an oft overlooked nuance that is in play every time a fielder makes a throw in virtually every baseball game. This nuance tells the umpires where to place the batter-runner(s) if the throw goes out of play based on where they were at one of two points in time, the time-of-the-pitch or the time-of-the-throw.

If you asked someone who understood most sports but didn't understand baseball to sort this out, they would probably guess that you award extra bases based on where the runner's were at the moment the ball goes out of play. This would be a logical guess but in baseball, this is never the case, I repeat, NEVER! Rather, **runners will be awarded bases from where they were at-the-time-of-the-throw, unless the throw is the first play by an infielder, then, it is based on where they were at-the-time-of-the-pitch.**

The logic behind this makes sense when you look at the history behind the rule. In the early years of baseball, all awards were made based on where the runners were at the time of pitch. This made it simple to administer base awards as the runners' base at the time of pitch is indisputable. Simple as this was, it was unfair to the offense on balls hit to the outfield because it negated any ground the runners could gain before the outfielder made the play and launched the throw. It allowed scenarios where the defense would benefit from bad throws because runners would be sent back to bases they would have passed had the ball stayed in play. The rule was wisely changed in 1931, specific to balls hit to the outfield, and called for the umpires to be governed by the position of the runners at the time-of-the-throw.

About a decade later, the same thought process lead to a similar change concerning second throws from the infield, that is, once again, the runners should be given credit for ground they may have gained while the first throw was being made. By the 1960s, the rule evolved to distinguish between the first "play" and the first "throw" meaning that if a fielder chased a runner back to a base for instance before throwing to a base, the move to chase the runner would be considered the first play and the first throw would actually be the second play…and that is how it reads now. **If the infielder's first play is a throw that goes out of bounds, then everyone advances two bases from where they were at the time of the pitch, otherwise it's is based on time of throw.**

Let me explain how this easily goes unnoticed in any game by looking at a routine grounder to short that is fielded cleanly but thrown wildly into the parking lot.

We know that it is 2 bases from time of pitch so the batter is awarded second and if there was a runner on second, he would be sent home. If there was a runner on first however and the defense attempted to turn a double play and the second baseman threw the relay into the parking lot, the runners get 2 bases from time of throw because that was the second throw, not the first. This is a bit of a trick example because the result is almost always the same, the batter-runner ends up on second and that's because when the second baseman made his throw, the batter-runner hadn't reached first yet but if he had, he would indeed be sent to third.

Technically, the basis for the award is different between that first throw and any subsequent one. This "time of pitch" rule makes it simple to award bases on routine plays and eliminates arguments about where the runners were, especially when there are multiple runners. That said, the rules do specify however, **that if all runners have advanced one base before the first throw, then indeed, all runners will receive bases from the time of throw.** The implication is that something happened to allow everyone to advance. Perhaps the fielder booted the ball and then made a throw to catch a runner rounding a base. This would be the first throw but certainly not the first play; that was when his hands of stone deflected the ball! This rarely happens but it is important to note the difference in timing. **First throw from infield: two bases from time of pitch; everything else, time of throw** (this includes the first throw from infield after all runners advance one base, second and subsequent plays from infield, all throws from the outfield).

If I haven't taken a simple ruling and completely confused you by now, in practicality, almost all infield throws that go out of play result in two bases from time of pitch and there are very few outfield throws that ever go AWOL, so in actuality, umpires are rarely called on to note the position of the runners at the time of throw. This is where awards can become controversial in amateur ball because with only two umpires, each with multiple responsibilities, there is a lot that needs to be watched and it can be very difficult to pinpoint with certainty where all the runners were at the exact moment the ball left an outfielder's hand.

Let's say there is a base hit to right and the right fielder is attempting a throw to third to get the runner from first and that throw goes out of play, everyone naturally follows the ball so who notices where the batter-runner was when the throw was released? Sure, the base umpire is watching to make sure the batter-runner touched first, but just because he registers that in his memory, it doesn't mean the timing relative to the throw registers because its importance at that moment isn't clear. Again, this happens far less frequently than you would imagine so it's not a mechanic that is second nature for most amateur umpires and besides, coaches are usually watching the ball like everyone else at the game so if bases were misappropriated, they don't even realize they have a bone to gnaw on with Blue.

Base running awards can be controversial in amateur ball where anything can happen and, because of unique field conditions around the playground, it might not be obvious when and where a ball is considered "dead." Hopefully I've made it clear how many bases are awarded and from what point in time.

It gets a little more complicated when there is more than one runner as I just mentioned because you have to know where all the runners are, but there is one more nuance to putting all the runners in the right place. What if the awards don't align with each other?

By that, I mean, what if proper administration of the rules, puts two runners on the same base? We know that can't happen so let me explain how it is handled and let's use an example. Let's say there is a runner on first and the batter hits a bloop into short right field and the 2nd baseman, center and right fielders all converge but don't make the catch. The batter-runner runs hard and makes a big turn so one of the fielders picks up the ball and turns and fires to first for a back pick but the ball goes wild. Since the batter-runner had already reached first, he would be awarded third, however, the guy on first, who was unsure if the ball would be caught, never made it to second by the time the ball was thrown. He too would be awarded third because at the time of the throw, you had two runners between first and second and they both can't be placed at third, so what do we do? **The rules say that when the ball goes out of play, no runner can advance beyond the base he is entitled to**. That means the runner who was originally on first is sent to third (a 2 base award) and the batter-runner only goes to second (a 1 base award).

Another way to think of this is that the **awards are applied to the lead runner first and trailing runners next**. This "no push" rule is not universal because there are times when one runner pushes another; for example, a first baseman obstructs a runner diving back to first on a pick off move, he will be sent to second and if there is a runner there, he will also move up one base. This caveat, no runner going beyond his entitled base, only applies when an award is applied to multiple runners.

If The Glove Fits...

In one of my examples testing knowledge of base awards, I mentioned a batted ball that is fielded with an illegal glove. As unusual as this is, let's cover it quickly.

While there are some requirements we covered in the pitching section, like no white or gray, the rules mostly address size and distinguish between three categories of mitts, a special one for the catcher, a special one for the first baseman and lastly, the mitts used by everyone else. Mitts are measured in height, web width and palm width so without going into all the details, the key number is the height which is usually on the label when you purchase the glove. Catcher's mitts may be up to 15.5 inches in height while all other mitts cannot be more than 12 inches. There are palm and web differences between first baseman's mitts and regular fielder's gloves but just like the bat situation, manufacturers have no incentive to make illegal gloves, so it's unlikely it is something that comes up in a game.

One other requirement for the catcher's mitt is that it must not be more than 38 inches in circumference. Go ahead, make my day and see what happens when you tell an umpire that the other team's catcher's mitt looks like it is 40 inches. In the rare event a player is caught using an illegal mitt at the professional level, the mitt is confiscated and all resulting plays stand; rules vary in amateur leagues and could result in awards to the offensive team and possibly a choice, like with catcher's interference, to take the penalty or the result of the play. What isn't specifically written in the rule book, but is implied, is that yes, only the catcher can use a catcher's mitt and only the first baseman can use a first baseman's mitt (6).

Appeals and the Mysterious 4th Out

We've been talking about handing out bases which we classified as "awards" to the offense and "penalties" for the defense. So what about the opposite, "penalties" to the offense and "awards" for the defense? The currency for these transactions is simply in the whole units known as "outs." For a lack of a better word, baseball is just weird in its handling of missed bases because I can't think of examples from other sports where the officials overlook an infraction until the offended team points it out. I have to conclude it is related to the uniqueness of baseball I highlighted earlier, that **it's the only game where the defense holds the ball and as such, it is their burden to put out the batter-runners**.

In fact, this burden has existed since the original Knickerbocker rules and includes even the most basic of obligations for the runners, touching their bases. Controversial as this is, players and coaches must be aware that proper mechanics by an umpire should not tip off the defense that a base was missed. It is common for a home plate umpire to simply not give a safe or out sign if he thinks the runner missed the plate, but he should ignore this and make a call. You heard me correctly!

Let me give you another example, a close play at first where the runner beats it out but doesn't touch the base. That's right - with the burden of proof on the defense, the umpire should simply make the safe call based on the assumption of a touched base as it is the defense's responsibility to point out that the base was missed. This is accomplished by an **"appeal"**, **which is defined as an act by the defense to claim violation of the rules by the offense.** There are appeals in most baseball games, you just don't realize it; when a runner is doubled off a base on a caught line drive for example; this is an appeal executed by the defense - throwing the ball to a fielder who steps on the base of the runner who left too early. **When these infractions are obvious to everyone on the field by the very nature of the play, they are accomplished in real time and require no explanation.**

When they are not completed in the course of the same play as the initial infraction they become a little more complicated because, if upheld, elements of the previous play must be unwound and can cause apparent runs to be taken off the board.

Let's look at how appeals are legally executed and the implications of the successful appeal.

First, there are 3 common appeals: **runner missed a base** (running in either direction), **failure to retouch properly** and **batting out of order**. I'm sure you may recall witnessing games when the defense believed the offense was guilty of one of these and there was a lot of anxiety and confusion associated with pulling off an appeal. Half the players were probably yelling at a fielder to throw the ball to a base and the other half were yelling at the pitcher to get the ball, go to the Set and step off the rubber and then the coaches put in their two cents, geesh...could everybody just calm down!

Before we get into the details of executing proper appeals, let me tell you about one of the greatest inventions in baseball, introduced at the high school level in recent years, the "Dead-ball" appeal. In high school, all the defense has to do is call time out and any coach or player on the field can address an umpire and simply verbalize the challenge, "the batter missed first base", "the guy left third too early", and voila, the umpire simply says yes or no and the game moves on. The appeal is after all a formality, so it makes no sense to me that it has to be acted out physically and is allowed to affect play at all. I suppose at the professional level it adds an element of drama and decorum to the proceedings, but in your average amateur game, it is largely unnecessary and not something players are taught because it's really not something that takes baseball skills, it's all procedure.

In fact, the whole get-the-ball-to-the-pitcher-so-he-can-step-off-to-appeal is largely unnecessary because **as long as the ball is still "live", the defense can simply appeal at the end of the play in question without involving the pitcher**. If time was granted or the ball left play, then yes, the appeal must involve the pitcher because **the only way the umpire is going to call "play" to re-start the game is if the pitcher, batter, and catcher are all in their proper positions**. When this is the case, the pitcher must set up in a legal pitching position on the rubber and then legally step off to execute the appeal. Let's quickly look at the procedure for appeals but not dwell on it, what's more important is how the preceding play is unwound.

1. When can the defense appeal?
    a. At the end of the action of the play in question while the ball is still live or...
    b. Before the next pitch after the ball has been put in play by the plate umpire.
    c. If the third out has been made, before all infielders cross the foul lines, not including the catcher. If he has not left his position, he is eligible to request the appeal. Outfielders? We don't care!
    d. If the appeal follows a game-ending play, it must be requested before all umpires leave the playing surface which implies it is okay to appeal after all the fielders have left fair ground.

2. When does the defense lose the right to appeal?
    a. If a pitch is made following the end of the play in question.
    b. If the pitcher balks before an appeal.
    c. If the ball is thrown out of play while making the appeal, it's an official botch job and no further appeal can be made.

3. How is the appeal executed?
    a. A fielder, with possession of the ball, legally tags the runner in question.

    b.   A fielder, with possession of the ball, steps on the base in question, including home plate.

    c.   And if not apparent, it is verbally made clear to the umpires what the defense is doing. i.e. a player who accidentally steps on the base with the ball in the course of action would not assumed to have been making an appeal. He must state his intention.

Do the Runs Count?

As much as I love the idea of the dead-ball appeal for its simplicity, there's really no reason why the live-ball appeal should cause such a fuss. The defense just needs to be aware that the runners might be tempted to steal a base while they are making the appeal because it is a live ball. Also, multiple appeals may be made on one play, as the Yankees did following the continuation of the George Brett pine tar game, but you obviously can't appeal the same runner twice for the same thing. And speaking of Mr. Brett, the real fun comes after an appeal is upheld and a runner is called out following a play when at least one run was scored. We can discuss endless examples of such plays that might be confusing but we don't need to because there are only a couple of facts that need to be established in order to sort it out quickly:

- Understand the difference between a force out and a "time play." Either the runner is out at a base he was forced to advance to or not, and then it's a time play, when the runner must cross the plate before the third out was made in order to count the run. Common example: runners on 1st & 2nd with one out, long fly to center, both runners tag and the throw goes to third. The runner from third will score if he crossed plate "in time" before the runner from second was tagged out going in to third.

- **If the out called on the appeal is not the third out, then there is nothing to debate as all runs scored on the play in question count, except of course for the appealed runner.**

- If the out on appeal is the third out then we have a few scenarios and this is where it can get tricky:

  1. Very important – **if the appealed third out was a force out, including first base, then NO runs can be scored on the play.** Think of your ordinary inning ending play and the same rules apply retroactively when the 3rd out is on an appeal.
  2. **No following runner can score.** This is an easy one, if a runner becomes the third out on appeal, his run as well as anyone who scored behind him will not count.
  3. **Preceding runners who scored before the appeal count if it is a time play** (or not a force).

There are endless examples but only three little rules: #1 and #2 are straightforward so that leaves #3 as the one to think about, the "time play."

For years, I thought that the preceding runs were evaluated theoretically one base at a time, based on how far the batter got before missing his base. So, in the example of the bases loaded triple where the batter missed second, I used to think that the runner from third's run would count but not the runners from first and second because if the batter only legally got one base then all runner's would retroactively be limited to one base as well…but I was very wrong! **As long as it is not a force play, all preceding runners are evaluated based on time-play rule which means they will all count because they obviously scored before the appeal takes place at the end of the play. The third out is not retroactive in terms of timing so all the runs scored by the non-appealed runners count.**

Given this, counting runs after an appealed out is not as complicated as it seems; using our example, the batter is the third out for missing second base but all three runs count because they crossed the plate before the third out was made on appeal. This is simple to apply because it results in an "all or nothing" ruling. If the batter hits one out of the park but misses first base, no runs can score but if he misses any other base, which is not a force out, it is a timing play and since all the runners crossed the plate before the appeal, they will all count...except the run for the knuckleheaded slugger who missed the base. Oh, and by the way, the reason the lead run on Brett's homer did not count was that this wasn't a missed base appeal, but use of illegal equipment which nullified, at the time, any and all results of the play.

Finally, the Fourth Out!

You can say that when a fielder makes an unbelievable play he went above and beyond the call of duty but there is actually a time when the defense really has to go above and beyond to prevent a run from scoring by recording a fourth out in an inning. No, this isn't a trick question involving a guy who reached because of a dropped third strike. It happens when the offense screws up and the defense has to appeal after a third out has already been made in order to take a run off the board.

Let's go back to that fairly common situation from a moment ago: runners on second and third with one out and the batter hits a fly to center and both runners tag up. The ball is caught in the outfield for the second out and the runner going in to third is thrown out for the third out. Remember I said that if the runner coming from third crosses home before the runner going to third was tagged out, his run will count? Well, let's say he did and it does. Simple - right? The run counts because it was scored before the 3rd out. But let's say the runner from 3rd left too soon. The only way the run will *not* count is if the defense makes the appeal for the fourth out of the inning. What this really amounts to is a play that has two third outs and the defense chooses to take the one that is to their advantage but no matter how you look at it, it's four outs.

That last example doesn't seem too far fetched because a double tag-up is a fairly common baseball play, so the defense is paying attention to the runners, but let me give you an example of a play that actually happing in the major league that caught the defense totally unaware of their 4th out burden.

It happened on April 12, 2009 in Arizona in a game between the DBacks and Dodgers. With Juan Pierre on second and Andre Ethier on third and one out, Dodger batter Randy Wolf lined out sharply to his counterpart, DBack's pitcher Dan Haren. Both runners broke on the liner so it was obvious to everyone, once the pitcher snared it for the second out, that an inning ending double play was imminent. Haren chose to go to second to double off Pierre, since his momentum was carrying him that way so he threw the ball to second baseman Felipe Lopez. All Lopez had to do was step on second base for the easy double play but instead, chose to casually track down Pierre who was half-way to third and dead to rights.

In the mean time, Ethier, who was breaking from third, just kept going home and, since the Dodger dugout was on the first base side of the field, had the presence of mind to touch the plate on his way by, which he did before Lopez caught up to Pierre. Was the third out of the inning a force play? No, that means it was a time play situation and the out on Pierre served as misdirection taking all attention off of Ethier, even though it was obvious to everyone in the park that he left early.

The DBacks proudly left the diamond after recording the third out not realizing they were leaving behind some unfinished business. An alert bench coach pointed out the scenario to Dodger skipper Joe Torre who came out to argue that the run should count. After an umpire conference, it was determined the run indeed counted because the DBacks failed to appeal that Either left early, for the fourth out; and as you learned earlier, because it was the end of the inning, Arizona lost the right to appeal when all infielders crossed the foul lines. You might never see a 4th out in your lifetime, but it does exist!

"Infielder Fly Rule" - Part III

I've segmented the discussion about the infield fly rule as it affects hitters, runners and fielders in slightly different ways. It should affect the fielders because they should always be trying to catch the ball but like the runners, they need to be trained to look for the call from the umpires so if the ball does hit the ground, they know if they have a force play on their hands or are required to tag a runner out. Just as an alert base coach should warn runners, the defense should always know when the IFR is in effect, **(runners on 1st and 2nd or bases loaded and less than two outs...**of course) and I am talking about everyone on the diamond, not just the infielders. Lets look how the IFR is called.

First things first, note that it is not called the infield "pop-up" rule but **"fly" rule which is defined as a ball that is hit in the air but is not a line drive or a bunt. A "line drive" is defined as a ball that is hit sharply towards a fielder without hitting the ground**. I think we all know what a line drive is so that shouldn't cause a problem when evaluating a ball for the IFR but what about the soft liner? Well, a liner is a liner so if the ball is hit mostly parallel to the ground, it should be considered a line drive and not subject to the IRF. A fly is a ball hit up in the air, so as soon as a ball appears to be on more of an up/down path then the IFR should be a consideration.

The next requirement for a potential IFR call is that **the ball must be able to be caught with "ordinary" effort** so it's fair to say it needs to be a routine play...but for whom?

I was once umpiring a game in an age-55 and over league and the second baseman was in his mid seventies and playing way back at the edge of the infield cut out. A pop-up was hit that landed on the dirt directly in front of him because he only gained a few feet of ground coming in but I ruled IFR. My argument was that the rule book doesn't say ordinary for an old guy or a guy with a sore ankle or maybe someone who has had a few too many cheeseburgers. The whole point of the IFR is to prevent unfair double plays when the batter does not get the job done; I say a routine pop-up in the direction of an infielder is not getting the job done.

That said, a subsequent review of the major league rule book **says "ordinary" should be defined as a play that can be made with "average skill" for someone in that league**.

Now, that doesn't mean all flies in the infield should be considered catchable. A low hanging pop-up that is heading for the dead zone behind the mound is a candidate for an infield single as are looping balls hit between fielders. An umpire can never predict the future and know exactly what will happen so he has to use his best judgment but also wait as long as he can to determine the right call. Yes, it must be a fly and yes it must be catchable with routine effort and the best way for the umpire to determine that is to wait for the ball to reach its apex. Once he sees the ball begin to drop, he should then evaluate the situation with fielders moving in to make the play and at that point, if there is any doubt it will be caught easily, the IFR should not be called.

This is a safe strategy because again, the point is to prevent unfair double plays and in most baseball games, that could only happen when it is obvious to everybody that it is an IFR and the runners hold. If it's not obvious to everyone, then the runner's job is to move off the base and be prepared to advance but also be able to get back to their base; this is smart base running. In these in-between cases, if the ball does hit the ground and the runners are doing their job, then most likely the defense will only get one out and it is quite possible they won't get anybody out. This is the crux of the rule, to protect the runners in an unfair situation but once the situation moves to a more equitable balance between offense and defense, let the action take precedence; this is the challenge the officials face when making, or quite often, not making the call.

My example with the seventy-five year old second baseman is an unusual situation of course so let's look at how it should play out at the highest level of the game, the pros.

There was a very controversial IFR call in the first round of the 2012 National League playoffs in a game between the Cardinals and the Braves. With the Braves trailing 6-3 in the bottom of the 8th inning, they had runners on first and second with one out when a high fly ball was hit into short left field. Okay, lets stop right here. Short left-field? Calling this rule the "infield" fly rule is a bit of a misnomer – it would be better to call it the "infield-*er*" fly rule because the application of the rule revolves around the fielders not the field itself. The rule book is somewhat contradictory about this because it says that for the purposes of the rule, **any outfielder who is positioned "in the infield" shall be considered infielders** but in the comments section it says that **the infield itself shall not be defined by "some arbitrary limitation such as the grass."**

The first statement implies the outfielders must be in the infield but the second statement says the infield that we all know is not the infield and redefines it as something more abstract by the following statement: **"the umpire must also rule the ball an infield fly, even if handled by an outfielder, if the ball could have been as easily handled by an infielder."**

Okay, so now we have established we can throw out the "infield" part of the "infield" fly rule but my new name won't work either because we can throw out the "infielder" part of the "infielder" fly rule. So what is left..."The Fly rule." Yes, the infield fly rule can be invoked on a ball fielded by someone other than an infielder in a place that is somewhere other than the infield. Once we remove these abstract boundaries, we can now go back to our example in the 2012 major league playoffs...

In an IFR situation, the Brave's shortstop Andrelton Simmons launched a high fly to short left field that drew the

Cardinal's left fielder Matt Holiday in and shortstop Pete Kozma out. Running on a slight angle towards the foul line, Kozma put his arms indicating "I've got it" and appeared ready to make the grab but quickly peeled off thinking Holiday called him off. To the delight of the Brave's home crowd, the ball fell to the ground in a classic case of "I've got it, you take it"…and everybody advanced.

The "hit" would load the bases with one out but what went unnoticed, as all eyes followed the ball towards the impending miscommunication between fielders, was that the left field umpire raised his arm to indicate infield-fly-rule.
Seeing Kozma gather himself under the ball, the batter was declared out. Instead of the bases loaded with one out, there was now two outs with runners on second and third. The rally, while not killed entirely, was snuffed out two batters later when Michael Bourn struck out to end the inning.

Timing is everything of course, so coming in the 8th inning of the inaugural one game elimination, created when baseball added an additional wild card team in 2012, the stakes couldn't have been higher. Once they realized what the call was, and correctly sensed the impending 6-3 loss, the Atlanta faithful let loose.

Reigning down their disapproval, as well as their bottles and cans, Braves fans created a 19 minute "reign delay" that, unbeknownst to them, allowed the Brave's to protest the game and be turned down in real time before the game resumed. In the post game press conference Atlanta manager Fredi Gonzales said he protested the game because he felt the play was not "ordinary", given the 50,000 screaming fans and playoff atmosphere. Joe Torre, the former acclaimed manager of 4th out fame was in the stands as a major league baseball executive vice president and ruled, on the spot, that since it was a judgment call by the umpire, that it could be caught with ordinary effort, the call, and game, was not subject to protest. Cardinal's manager Mike Matheny made the post game comment that foreshadows my analysis of the play: "But our

guys would have made this a whole lot easier if we make the play, and they make that play 99 times out of a hundred. It just didn't happen that time."
Here's how I see it...

1.   Was it a fly? Yes, obviously – check!
2.   Putting aside arbitrary definitions of the infield, was the ball as easily catchable by an infielder as an outfielder? In this case both Holliday and Kozma could have caught it so yes – check!
3.   The play must be able to be accomplished with routine effort by an average major league fielder. Before peeling off, Kozma had his arms up calling for it as he settled in for the catch. It wasn't going to require a dive or an over the shoulder catch. It did require a fairly long run but it was not extraordinary for a major leaguer – check!
4.   And what about that left field umpire. He waited as long as he could to apply the best judgment possible and when all of the first three elements listed above came together, he raised his arm and invoked the IFR...and as though on cue, just as he did, Kozma peeled off and the ball hit the ground, an unfortunate situation for the Braves but fortunate for the Cards.

Another interesting element of this play is that the IFR was called by an umpire who normally wouldn't be there. Regular season games are played with four umpires but because it was the playoffs, there were two additional umpires, stationed on the outfield foul lines, one of whom made the call. In the debate that followed the play, TV commentator and former major league pitcher Ron Darling made the great observation that "extra umpires mean extra calls." It appears that none of the other umpires had their arms up to signal IFR so it seems they felt this ball was out of the abstractly defined infield or that it was not an ordinary play. Separated by perspectives on either side of the fence, it was only the outfield guy who ruled IFR. Darling's subtext was that you had an overzealous umpire trying to grab any opportunity to make a call, as outfield umpires don't get much action, but in a post game statement, umpire Sam Holbrook said the following: "I saw the shortstop go back and get underneath the ball where he would have had an ordinary effort...and that's why I called the infield fly"; how can you argue with that?

Given the wonderful thing that is 20-20 hindsight, I can only conclude that the umpires, or should I say, *the umpire,* Sam Holbrook, got this one right as the rule is written, the *letter* of the law, if not the *spirit.* This ball could only be called the IFR at the highest level of the game because the amateur game is not played on such a scale that a ball this far into the outfield could be reached with ordinary effort by the shortstop.

On the other hand, I feel this violates the spirit of the rule because it is written to prevent an unfair double play and as we saw, once the ball hit the ground, the defense wasn't even able to get one out. If it were a valid IFR rule play, the Cardinals should have been able to force out one of the runners, in my opinion, and if they couldn't, something isn't quite right. This incidentally would have incited an all out riot beyond the bottle throwing; you would have had a situation where the enforcement of a rule to protect the offense would have lead to the defense turning a double play. So what are we to do?

While I would like to cleverly say baseball should shorten the name of the rule simply to "The Fly Rule", it really is an infield fly rule so the language of the rule should be changed to not be so vague about the demarcation between infield and outfield. It's smart to not have the infield defined by an arbitrary marking, like the infield cutout, but there is a tipping point the further into the outfield the ball travels and I think this needs to be addressed. With regards to an outfielder catching the ball, I think they should add to the wording "as easily handled by an infielder" with something that specifies location on the field like..."as easily handled by an infielder if in the normal range/domain of that position." This would allow the umpires to ask themselves "is that ball more towards the shortstop or outfielder?" and if the answer is "outfield", then it would not be an IFR and in the case of the Braves-Cardinals playoff game, it would not have been called.

The rules, as currently written, try to have it both ways, calling the batter automatically out, but then saying the defense has to catch the ball. A better solution that I think would make sense at the amateur level is to simply declare the infield fly rule a dead-ball. You might think this is drastic but guess what, this rule is more or less already in effect. **The rules of baseball prohibit a player from intentionally dropping a ball in order to get additional outs**. I've seen many line drives hit at a middle infielder and they let it hit their glove and fall to the ground in and effort to slyly turn a double play. In these cases I've done what the rules call for, call time out and **declare the batter out and keep the runners on their base(s).**

The effect of the IFR is more or less the same, keeping everyone put with the caveat that the runners may advance at their own risk. Eliminating the option to run for the sake of preventing confused players from running into outs, and again, having a reverse effect of the intent of the rule, seems to me a wise trade off. The bottom line is the batter didn't get the job done and if the umpire determines a catch can be made with ordinary effort, then it really doesn't matter that the ball was not caught, the runners were protected and that is the point of the rule. Besides, the umpire can't predict the future, like when all of a sudden the infielder loses the ball in the sun, so let's limit the madness! In my opinion, the rule could be bulletproofed with a little clarification about *where* it can be called. With all the crazy base running that takes place in the amateurs, a dead-ball would save a lot of trouble and guarantee the rule, and call, accomplishes what it sets out to.

Section IV Footnotes

(1) Speaking of snow cones, I beg you to search Youtube for comedian Brian Regan's bit about free snowcones in little league...grape is good too!

(2) Bruno Block (1855-1937) from Wisconsin Rapids, WI, played 1907-1914 for Washington Senators, Chicago WhiteSox, Chicago Chi-Feds. Brandon Tripp (born 1985) is a current (2013) minor league player for the St. Paul Saints (AA).

(3) Including the ill-fated "Disco Demolition Night" at the old Comiskey Park, July 12, 1979. The premise was to blow up disco records between games of a doubleheader as part of a backlash against the popularity of disco music, reflecting the punk-rock rebellion of the day. Long story short, the fans rioted (very "rock n roll"), the White Sox forfeited game two of the double header, and in 2013, Daft Punk's "Get Lucky" is a huge 70's inspired disco hit.

(4) Google "Steve Bartman" if you don't know what I'm talking about...

(5) I love the movie "A League of Their Own", especially for the scenes at Doubleday Field in Cooperstown – did I ever tell you about the one I hit out of there? Anyway, there is a scene in the movie where Madonna's character, "All the Way" Mae Mortabito makes a catch using her hat. This bugs me every time I see it because it's against the rules.

(6) "Bill Buckner" is not a swear word. Regarding his ill-timed error in game 6 of the 1986 World Series, you can blame his first baseman's mitt more than his

creaky ankles. The mitt was so worn in and flexible that the pocket had no stiffness whatsoever. Moving to his left to field the ball, and bringing his glove hand (right) down, the pocket flapped closed and over-shot the ball because it had no rigidity at all. Haters will argue his back-up, Dave Stapleton, would have made the play but lets face it, it was fate; hell, "Oil Can" Boyd would have made the play. Anyway, Buckner was a great player who had a great career. Without his efforts, the '86 sox wouldn't have been in the World Series.

Section VI – Blues Clues

Earl Weaver, John Adams and The 5 Stages of Grief

I once had the pleasure of working a high school baseball game at Petco Park in San Diego, home of the Padres, and as sure as urban legend has it, the sign marking the entrance to the umpire's dressing room was subtitled in braille. I know it's just a case of the Padres complying with laws that make life a little easier for our sightless friends but it serves as a taunting reminder of the old Earl Weaver story about one of the famously cranky manager's frequent run-ins with the Blue (1).

Stomping off the field following a dust up, Weaver threatened to go check the rule book to settle a matter but the ump called his bluff and told him he could use his, right there on the field. Hell bent on having his say, Weaver shot back "That's no good – I can't read braille!" Nothing is more emblematic of American virtue than owning the final word and nothing is more deeply rooted in our founding fathers' idealism than a healthy mistrust of a single authoritative figure with absolute power, so when a manager springs out of the dugout to argue a call, it might as well be Lexington and Concord all over again. I can see a perturbed John Adams now, making his opening statement following a close call at the plate:

> "It is one thing to turn the other cheek, but to lie down in the ground like a snake and crawl toward the seat of power in abject surrender, well, that is quite another thing. And I have no stomach for it, sir! No stomach at all! Facts are stubborn things so I say to you before God and country, that man was safe on the home base!" (2)

There's just one problem though, freedom-of-speech, rule-of-law, and due-process might be treasured institutions, the bedrock of democracy, but at the end of the day there's no finer example of tyrannical rule than that of a baseball umpire, so the call stands Mr. President. **The rules of baseball**

clearly state that an umpire's decision, which involves judgment, is final and that no player or coach shall object to such decision.

Baseball's pace and tempo naturally makes room for these entertaining side-shows but you can also go the other way and say that they're an embarrassing display, the Ugly American in his element, loud, demeaning and self-serving. Either way, they rarely cause a call to be reversed, mostly all they do is speed-up the distraught manager's passage through the five stages of grief, which might just be another example of the ingenious design of baseball. Let's look at a typical "argument" following a close play at second:

Coach:	"HE MISSED THE TAG!"	(1. Denial)
Ump:	"No, he tagged him on the leg"	
Coach	"THAT'S HORRIBLE!"	(2. Anger)
Ump:	"He got him on the leg"	
Coach:	"Can you ask for help"	(3. Bargaining)
Ump:	"No, it's my call"	
Coach:	"You're killing me Blue…"	(4. Depression)
Ump:	"Sorry, can't help ya"	
Coach:	Slinks slowly back to dugout	(5. Acceptance)

Sure, the coach can seize the moment, or should I say super-seize it to "make a scene" if he senses it's a good time for it, perhaps stoking the fire with "that's two today you've blown" and then it's game on. This tactic will surely impart a calculated and palpable effect on the game but before I even start down this bumpy road and explore his motivation and madness, I need to stop because this is the problem. When we think of baseball umpires, we think of wrong calls, arguments and Earl Weaver. I take no issue with any of that as they have their place in the game and that's why I don't need to discuss them here, because they have their place in the game. Let me explain.

Until the game is perfectly officiated by blue hover-bots, questionable calls will stick as surely as batters will swing and miss because umpires are human. I know, you've heard that one before and the only reason I bring it up is to point out that this has been a constant throughout the history of the game and even though major league baseball is embracing instant replay, umpire judgment will long be the final say in the vast majority of baseball. Schools and amateur associations simply don't have the resources to implement replay, blue-bots or even a two-dollar smart phone app that surely must be in development. As far as this portion of the book is concerned, the whole topic is simply a red herring, putting negative focus on the occasional human error and diverting our attention away from the real matter at hand, the rules and the discipline of umpiring.

What I would rather accomplish is to share basic umpire mechanics and then, all things being equal, discuss the most important physical and intangible factors that influence calls when they're so close they can go either way. I can't possibly explain to you why any umpire boots a call more than I can explain to you how any infielder boots a grounder but we can have an intelligent baseball discussion about fundamentals can't we? Before the pitch, did the guy think about what he would do on a ball hit to his left, or to his right? Did he take a good angle? Did he set up properly? Was he focused or did he just lollygag out there dreaming of an icy post-game snowcone on a hot and humid day? I'm talking about both guys.

I'm sure you've watched enough baseball to pick out the best players on the field based on a quick assessment of their fundamentals and it's no different with umpires who are generally evaluated on about twenty different criteria. Yes, judgment is one of these but that hardly matters because if an umpire is solid on most others, you can guarantee that his judgment is pretty good. It means he's working hard out there; he's professional, he knows the rules, he hustles, he communicates with his partner, he positions himself well, has good timing, and so on.

So what does that mean to you? Well, as a serious baseball fan, when you notice the umpires running around out there, it should make as much sense to you as a pitcher covering first base on a grounder to the right side and it should be apparent to you that they are doing their job well or not before a tough call ever comes down the pike. If you're on the field in any capacity, the best way to gain leverage with the officials is to be in a position to evaluate and audit them, to call their bluff so to speak when the stuff hits the fan, which it surely will. Not just to argue a call for arguments sake but to gain favor by speaking their language and asking the right questions. I can tell you from personal experience as a player, that with zero knowledge of the rule book or umpire mechanics, I used to tactlessly argue check-swings, balks, balls and strikes as though I was Johnny Cochran in the trial of the century(3). Surely the glove didn't fit because I often had no idea what I was talking about which always seemed to keep me stuck on stage two of the grief thing, anger. I was more like Jackie Chiles than Johnny Cochran. Don't be that guy! And if you still must think of the umpires as the spawn of Satan, well then, humor me and heed the words of Don Vito Corleone, "keep your friends close, but your enemies closer."

Answering to a Higher Authority

If you disregard the rule differences between the amateur and pro game, baseball is baseball, that is, the game is more or less played the same way from little league on up to the majors and the same holds true for officiating with respect to mechanics. The most notable difference you'll see from game to game is the number of umpires on the field but whether there are two, three, four or more, each system is based on and built upon the core principals established with two-man mechanics.

But before we ask "how many umpires does it take to change a lightbulb?" I want to take a step back and quickly touch on their larger role. Of course their primary job is to call ball/strike, fair/foul, safe/out and so on, to enforce the rules, but underlying all of this, they have a larger obligation to uphold the integrity of the game which formally begins when they enter the confines of the field and ends when the last umpire exits that gate. Think of the Umpire-in-Chief as the captain of a ship the moment he steps on the field at which point the game has set sail and he is responsible for its efficient operation and safe return. All persons on board, including officers and crew, other shipboard staff members, passengers, guests and pilots, are under the captain's authority and are his ultimate responsibility.

In a baseball game, this includes points of emphasis that includes, but is not limited to, safety, minimizing risk, good sporting behavior by all participants and fans, pace of play, equipment compliance as well as authority to rule on any point not covered by the rules, and to rectify any situation following umpire judgment that has placed either team at a disadvantage. I realize that's a mouthful but whether the game you're watching metaphorically resembles a dinghy or the mother ship, the last thing an umpire does is make that call that sends your blood pressure through the roof. I bring this up only to point out that at any moment, an umpire's focus may be distributed across these other distractions that might not be apparent to everyone else and certainly vary greatly from level to level on up to pro baseball.

Grander vs. Grandeur

Pro sports are one thing, where winning really is everything and the results are what they are, for the benefit and enjoyment of all as entertainment and for the professional pursuits of the participants and those with financial interests, preserved for posterity. Not so in the amateur ranks.

Naturally, wins and losses are an important measure in our culture and psyche but lets have a moment of honesty if we can; amateur sports are about one of two things, human development or recreation and that's it, not self-actualization. At their best, sports are a place to learn the value of teamwork and fair play, sacrifice for the common good and perseverance, and if not that, well then, for the exercise and fun, beer and snowcones.

Certainly there are times when success at the amateur level carries a grander importance on its back for a player, coach or institution but most of the time that weight is only importance of grandeur. This distinction between the pro and amateur virtue has unique implications to baseball because of the way it is officiated. Other sports are chock full of their largely indisputable off-sides, shot-clock violations, and icings as the officials and players move freely around the playing surface but baseball umpires use abstract judgment in a very controlled environment to dispense their brand of justice.

You probably agree with this statement because surely you've witnessed perceived acts of vengeance from a spiteful umpire, cloaked in black, sticking it to somebody on a wide strike three called out with great passion and purpose as payback for an earlier insult, "vendetta e morte!"

Sure, it happens, but I'm here to tell you that more often than not, it's not personal but rooted in an honest effort to keep things competitive in the interest of good sportsmanship or dare I say, to stay true to the lofty objectives and purer aspirations of amateur sports. That's right, I said it, we often make calls with a larger purpose than just the call itself but you didn't hear that from me.

Certainly when the competition is serious and winning and losing is on the line, every amateur umpire is trying to be as professional as possible with a complete commitment to unadulterated objectivity and impartiality. Amateur sports provide an awful lot of game time where winning and losing isn't on the line however and this is where a baseball umpire has a lot of leeway to keep it moving and competitive. I won't extend this lecture but when you see a call you don't agree with, the umpire could just be granting an extra swing to a bench player on his only at bat of the week or helping out a struggling pitcher for a team that's getting clobbered. Whatever the reason, the umpire knows what he is doing in an effort to keep the whole darn baseball train from careening off the tracks.

Note that this isn't limited to little tyke baseball or to amateur baseball at large, umpires at all levels have a sliding scale of motivation to toggle the benefit of the doubt on calls that are close enough to go both ways, the only difference being the degree of subtly. This also doesn't mean umpires don't make mistakes or don't get personal at times; but, when a call does grab your attention, it is possible there is something else going on and the ump is adhering to this unwritten responsibility to maintain sportsmanship, which includes paying attention to competitive balance. One last word on this, while I've talked specifically about balls and strikes here, there are calls all around the diamond that are in that can-go-both-ways zone and they do.

How Many Umpires Does it Take to Change a Bulb?

So, that's a brief missive on my philosophy about amateur sports and specifically my take on officiating baseball; just something to think about the next time you're watching a game. Now let's look at umpiring systems.

How many umpires does it take to change a lightbulb anyway? None, those guys are all blind so lights don't matter! Thank you, I'll be appearing here all week long…where was I? Yes, major league baseball uses four-man crews during the regular season, minor leagues typically use three and high school, college and most other amateur leagues use two umpires for regular season games. Each system builds upon the previous one so we'll start with two-man but before we do that

I want to add that it's also possible you might come across a game with only one umpire. There isn't much of a system here as the guy has to cover the whole field but I will point out that **the rules of baseball say it is okay for the umpire to stand behind the pitcher or take any position on the field.** This isn't just an improvisation reserved for a dad who fills in when the ump doesn't show and in fact was used during a major league spring training game in 2013.

After starting plate umpire Seth Buckminster broke his left hand on a pitch that hit and deflected off Albert Pujols, rather than hold the game up, the ubiquitous Tim McClelland, yes that same guy from the Brett and Sosa bat epics, called balls and strikes from behind the mound while one of his crew changed into his plate gear. It was only for four batters and he wouldn't have done it in a regular season game but technically, he could, the rules say it's legal.

Blue Man Groups

You know from watching baseball that in a two man system you have one umpire who covers the bases (U1) and one who calls balls and strikes behind the plate (PU), that's right, "P-U", "grow up!"

The separation of duties might seem obvious but there are divisions of labor out there you probably don't realize exist. When there are no base runners, U1 starts out on the line behind first base but responsibility for calling catch/no catch for balls in the outfield is PU most of the time. The standard rotation when the ball is hit is that U1 comes into the infield to track and stay ahead of the batter-runner moving around the bases so you should notice PU hustle towards the mound to gain as much ground as possible to get the best view of the play in the outfield. While it might be obvious to everyone a catch was made, you should hear PU vocalize "out" loud enough so his partner, who was making sure the runner touched first, knows the ball was caught. The effect here is that the guy furthest away from the ball makes the call which might not make sense but note that this is for routine plays.

If there is a "trouble ball" in the outfield and by that I mean a ball that might be caught below the waist or has fielders converging, or an outfielder going back, then U1 will run to the outfield to make the call and PU will track the runner. You won't notice PU because your attention will be on the ball but when the throw comes into second, he will magically materialize all the way out at second base to make the call.

The fully realized rotation has PU tracking the batter-runner all the way to third but if it is an attempt for an inside the park home run, believe it or not, it's U1's job to get all the way back to the plate to make the call, which he should be able to do in the interim. This holds true only on trouble balls hit from the center fielder towards right, anything to left, trouble or not, is always tracked by PU and remember, I'm talking about the situation with nobody on base.

Another thing you might not notice when no one is on, is that on ground balls, PU should follow the runner to about the 45 foot mark on the first base line so he can watch for the first baseman's foot coming off the bag or for a swipe tag, not so he can provide a second opinion on a safe/out call. Since the first baseman often turns his back to U1 when fielding a wide throw, blocking his vision, it is a perfectly good mechanic for U1 to not make a call, point to PU and ask, "Do you have a tag?" Or "Did he pull his foot?" You should notice that even in the pros, with a four-man crew, the PU gains ground to first although pro umpires rarely seem to need to go to each other for help on those. A sure sign PU is not hustling is when he makes no effort to run up the line but be aware that when there are runners on base, he has to stay closer to home for a potential play there. PU always has this responsibility so it's always valid for a coach to ask U1 if he can get help from PU on these plays but it's awfully hard to assist with certainty from 90 feet away. Again, PU can't help on safe/out calls but he sure can on tags and a pulled foot.

Experienced umpires have non-verbal cues worked out to tell their partner they have additional information in these situations so after reaching the 45 foot mark, if PU doesn't turn and quickly retreat he may just stand there and stare down his partner, telling him he saw something that U1 might not have seen. This works both ways as U1 might do the same for any of PU's calls. Regardless, **if a coach doesn't ask an umpire to get help and the primary umpire agrees to ask for help, the other umpires are not obligated to interject.** The expectation that one umpire will preemptively override another is overwhelmingly problematic; how would that fly in your work environment?

Two-Man, Runners on Base, U1 Inside

Once there are runners on base in the two-man system, U1 will take a position behind the mound on the first base side when there are runners on first, or first and third, or on the second base side of the mound in all other cases. Once U1 stations himself "inside", the responsibility for outfield catches shifts to him because he now has a better view of the outfield with one exception, on either side of the field, a ball hit that has either the left or right fielder charging towards their respective foul lines. With the fielders facing the foul line and potentially diving, the best view flips back to PU so he will call off U1 on these balls because he has the better angle. This outfield coverage is called "the cone" for U1 because of the V shape of his area of responsibility.

I will confess that based on personal experience, the biggest challenge in the two-man system is on pickoff moves to first base because U1 is behind the mound, about fifty feet away from first base with a less than ideal angle for the view of the runner who is diving back towards the base, away from you. Baseball can be a game of inches which is problematic when you are so far away trying to pinpoint the hand reaching for a base that might be partially covered with dirt. Add to that the possibility that the first baseman's body might be blocking your view and the need to judge two different focal points at the same instant - the position of the runner's hand on the base and the fielder's tag on the runner's body – and you have a lot to sort through.

On top of that, in the moment that the pitcher spins as you're following the ball to first, your brain is still processing the move for a balk and you also need to note if he stepped off the rubber because it changes the base award from one to two bases if the throw goes out of bounds or might be a balk if he doesn't release the ball. Before any of that happens, you will be rifling through your mental rolodex for all the plays that could happen next, a bunt, a steal, a double play ball, a check swing, etc.

The simple pickoff move proves to be a both fast and busy test and when the dust settles, it still might be hard to tell from your disadvantaged point on the field if the runner is back on the base or an inch off of it. My safeguard is that I have to be certain he is out before I ring him up because the burden of proof is on the defense, a runner is innocent until proven guilty in my courtroom. It's a bad habit for an umpire to call outs because the runner seemed out, so it should be clear beyond a reasonable doubt. Some umpires go the other way and call an out whenever possible and this takes us back to the last section where I talked about plays so close they can be reasonably called both ways. If I error on the side of the runner, I know it's not exactly cool that the pitcher made a nice move and I didn't see it well enough to be sure he was out but he, the pitcher, did let him get there in the first place so again, the runner is his burden.

The key for an accurate call on these plays is for the umpire to go slow and take a second or two to let the play register in his brain, something you can't speed up. It's not a lot of time but it can be the difference in making the right call or being tricked by what you saw initially, a throw that is in time yet the tag missed the runner, or a dive back to the base that beats the ball yet the runner's hand is not on the base. A call that is too fast will be stale and irrevocable two seconds later after all the facts become apparent. I'll say it a few times as it bears repeating, the single most important aspect of umpiring is timing and I'm talking about the difference of about two seconds on any call.

Running Away From Home

Once there are runners on base and U1 is inside, he will handle most calls at all bases except home from his position starting out on either side of the mound. Once the ball is put in play however, with the need to make calls at multiple bases, he will camp out in a space known as the working-zone, a triangular space behind the mound, the base of which extends out towards first and third, and the point being about twenty feet from second base. This allows him to gain ground towards any base without wandering so far that he can't quickly retreat for a secondary play at another base; the idea here is that angle takes importance over distance. When possible, PU will run away from home in order to help out in situations where there is no immediate possibility of a play at the plate. Understanding these PU rotations is the key to the two-man system. There are four potential PU rotations:

1.   Runner on 1st or 1st & 3rd, clean hit to outfield

With the possibility of the runner going from first to third on a hit, PU moves up to meet him there while U1 stays behind the mound to handle a back pick at second or a play on the batter-runner at first or second. If a throw gets loose and the lead guy continues towards home, PU will follow him there on the fair side of the third base line. First-and-third is effectively the same situation as a runner on first as there can be no play at the plate on the guy scoring from third so PU just has to make sure he watches him touch home on his way to third.

206

With runners on base, you should notice umpires giving signs to each other anytime there is a new batter or anytime a runner advances and the situation changes. These signals remind the umpires how many outs there are and what rotation is in play. In this case you should see PU indicate outs and then point to third base, indicating if there is a clean hit, he will rotate to third. U1 will acknowledge and perhaps indicate that he will stay where he is by pointing to the ground or toward first base.

2. Runners on 1st & 2nd, possible tag-up on fly ball to outfield

Since there is no reason to stay at home on this play, PU will rotate to third for a play on the lead runner while U1 watches both tag-ups and hangs back for a play on either runner at second. I'll talk a little bit more about this play in a moment when I discuss base touches and tag-ups but U1 has both. This is also an infield-fly-rule situation which PU will indicate by touching the brim of his cap and indicating the number of outs before indicating he will rotate to third.

3. Runner on 1st who is safe at 2nd on a double play attempt and proceeds to 3rd

This is a very uncommon situation because usually when a runner beats the throw to second, there is no play on the batter-runner at first. If there is a relay and the runner takes off for third, PU will meet him there while U1 focuses on the call at first. This is essentially the same rotation as situation number one described above, only that the ball didn't leave the infield.

4. Rundowns

Again, if there is no chance of an immediate play at the plate, PU will hustle up to first or third, depending on where the runner is floundering so he and his partner can box him in, that is, have an umpire both in front of him and behind him so together, they can't miss viewing a tag which can be a problem when the play is moving away from an umpire. If there are multiple runners trapped and all hell is breaking loose in terms of rundowns, both U1 and PU have to act calmly and not over commit to a base, especially U1 who has multiple bases to cover.

5. Force-play slides

I've talked about segregation of duties, the "cone" and outfield coverage, rotations and tricky plays like pickoffs, and the next thing we need to cover is something that differs significantly between the pro and amateur game, slide rules.

You might recall that in the section about the runner, I explained how amateur baseball prizes safety and there are strict slide rules that don't allow the runner to take out a fielder like you see in pro ball. Double-play balls, to begin with, are a serious challenge for U1 because he has to monitor two plays in rapid succession while rotating 180 degrees, and noting a few other facts along the way; there is safe/out of course, but there is also the transfer of the ball, the fielder's contact at the base and also the runner's slide or non-slide.

This last element is where U1 gets help from PU. With a runner only on first and a ground ball to the infield, you might not notice, but if PU is doing his job, he should be making a b-line for the mound because it's his job to stay with the slide after U1 turns to follow the ball. This "force-play slide rule" is a priority in high school and most amateur baseball so if the runner does something illegal, slide beyond the base to make contact during the turn or pop-up in front of the shortstop, PU should emphatically call time and kill the play, calling the runner out for interference and the batter-runner out as well. U1 always reserves the right to make this call and probably will be the one to make it if there is no relay to first, but once there is, it is PU's responsibility to call interference at second base.

Refer back to the section on the runner to refresh yourself on how interference is judged on the force-play slide rule but I will repeat here, **there is no rule that says the runner ever has to slide, just that he cannot interfere.** Again, like with tags and a pulled foot at first, when there are additional runners on base, you won't see PU gain ground towards second but he still has the responsibility to watch the play. If you're watching a pro game with four umpires, even though the pro rule is more liberal, it is still possible for a runner to interfere so U2 will watch the entirety of the slide and relay without ever turning towards first because U1 is there.

6. Base touches and tag-ups

The last ever-present responsibility I would like to talk about in the two-man system has to do with base touches and tag-ups; it's simple, U1 takes first and second base while PU has third and home and their heads should be on a swivel to make sure they see every single touch.

I have to say that I can't imagine anything else in sports that takes up so much of an official's attention and yields so few violations which when they do happen, usually aren't noticed and appealed by the defensive team. The only thing I will say about missed bases is that if discovered, they're "gift" outs served up on a silver platter because they are completely inconsequential, that is, there is no benefit to missing a base, unless the runner cuts a corner to shave distance off his trek, but that would be obvious to everyone. To prove my point, **the rule book specifies that when a base comes loose, a following runner is considered good if he is judged to have touched the spot where the base was;** this is the rule book's way of invoking the horseshoes and hand-grenade rule, close is good enough.

Tag-ups on the other hand are a very different story for two very good reasons. First, the runner has something to gain by leaving early, and second, because of the distance between

209

the ball and the runner. I'm always amused that fans in the stands or a coach in the dugout think they have a better view of a close play, looking through a fence from a hundred-and-something feet away, than the umpire right on top of it, but on tag-ups, they probably do, especially on the third base side of the field where you are nicely lined up to see the catch and the runner's separation from the base.

There are several problems on tag-ups, the first is that the umpires don't necessarily have great angles or sightlines to the runner(s), on top of the distance problem, especially on balls to right, and secondarily, in the two man system, umpires have multiple responsibilities that might make seeing all tag-ups (or touches) impossible.

Regarding the first issue, even in a four-man crew, the responsibility for the tag-up may still sit with PU who has to view a catch that can be three hundred-plus feet down the right-field line and quickly refocus on third base. In fact, I just saw a game at Yankee Stadium where an Angel runner was called out for leaving third base early yet the replay showed he clearly waited until the ball was touched by the outfielder. Even more revealing than that replay was the ensuing argument where you could read Angel manager Mike Scioscia's lips eloquently asking the plate umpire "what the bleep were you looking at?" About a week later, MLB announced plans to implement instant replay using a similar process to the NFL where the head coach, or in the case of baseball, the manager will have an option of challenging a call on the field. Instant replay will not be used for balls and strikes thankfully but this tag-up play is a good argument why it can be of help for other calls around the diamond, regardless of how you feel about replay in general.

Regarding multiple responsibilities in two-man, while **the runner can legally take off the instant the fielder touches the ball,** if the umpire responsible for the tag-up also has responsibility for the catch, he has to wait a few seconds to see what happens after the ball clunks Canseco on the head before he can turn his attention to the runner.

Seriously, if there is a dive or a tricky catch amidst converging fielders or a juggle, which I've seen, by the time an umpire is sure the ball was caught and properly transferred, the runner is long gone from the base so he won't know with certainty if the runner left early and he will have to make his best guess based on where the runner was when he finally locked sight on him. That's right, I said "guess"; imagine how early a runner has to leave before an umpire can guess with assurance that he left early. My point is that these plays are a big challenge for the umpires so if the runners leave a little early, there is a good chance they'll get away with it.

Another one that might sneak by everyone is when there are multiple tag-ups. While PU ever only has to patrol third base for tag-ups, U1 has to watch runners from both first and second so if we look at a deep fly with the bases loaded, there's a lot going on. U1 has to track the ball to the outfielder, make sure there is a legal catch, watch the runner on second tag-up properly, watch the runner on first tag-up properly, wait to see where the throw from the outfield goes and then possibly hustle towards third base for the play and make sure he stays out of the way of the throw and cutoff man. This can be like that scene from "Dirty Harry" when Lieutenant Callahan is trying to figure out if he has any bullets left "...to tell you the truth, in all this excitement I kind of lost track myself." Very often, both the umpire and the defensive team will forget about the trailing runner and I've seen the guy from first cruise into second base after going half way and nobody notices he didn't tag because "in all the excitement" they followed the throw to get the leading runner. When there are only runners on first and second, U1 will get help from PU as I described earlier and take third; with runners on second and third, PU will stay at home of course and U1 will slide down to third, but he still has to note both tag-ups.

In general, the two-man system does its best to cover all the bases, pun intended, but it is sometimes impossible to see everything so it's important the umpires remember what their priorities are. Ball/strike, safe/out, fair/foul and catch/no catch will always take precedence over base touches or tag-ups in the two man system. It is much more important for example, for PU to track a ball down the right field line to get fair/foul correct than to notice the runner's touch at third once the ball drops. His responsibility to help out U1 for a pulled foot or swipe tag at first is also much more important than noticing an uncontested runner touch the plate.

Three and Four-Man

Three-man is typically used in higher level college and upper-level minor league pro baseball and allows for fuller coverage of the field on trouble balls to the outfield because with nobody on base, there are umpires positioned behind first, U1, and third base, U3, on the foul lines. Rather than relying on PU to track a trouble ball to left-field, U3 will go out there. As soon as either U1 or U3 goes to the outfield to track a ball, the system reverts back to the two man process since once an umpire goes to the outfield he stays there until the end of the play, no matter two, three or four man system.

Having three umpires is better than two but it's still one less umpire than bases so you'll see more running around than with the two-man system. Since plays at first base are so common, the three-man system does it's best to keep U1 there but also guarantee that there's always an umpire in front and behind every runner. If you think of PU as anchored to the plate (with exceptions) and U1 anchored at first (with exceptions), the three-man system has U3 doing most of the running around. With nobody on he starts out behind third base but on most plays will run a straight line to the second base cut-out to be ready for the batter-runner's arrival. Once there are base runners, he'll take a position on the inside, just to the left or right of second base which allows him to be at second base for force outs and steals and easily track runners to third as well. When he covers third U1 will follow any trailing runners to second base. There are exceptions but in general, just think of U3 as the guy that has to cover two bases most of the time while U1 and PU stay at first and home respectively.

When we think of umpire systems, we tend to think of their importance by base coverage in the infield but in reality, the more umpires you have, the biggest advantage is how much extra outfield coverage you get, which shouldn't be underestimated.

In two-man, only one umpire is available to go out, that's U1 and only from center to right. In three-man, two umpires are available to go out, U1 takes the center fielder breaking towards right while U3 takes the centerfielder breaking in or towards left. Logically then, four-man gives us one additional umpire available to work the outfield and provides the luxury of starting out with an umpire in center field, U2, known as "the rabbit" because of all the hopping around he'll do. That's right, you may not have noticed but when there are no runners on base, U2 will be positioned in shallow center field. His job will be to take all trouble balls in the cone which you might recall is the space from left fielder all the way to right fielder. If either of those guys breaks towards the line, it will be the first base umpire (U1) or third base umpire's (U3) ball and he (U2) will hustle in towards second for any play there.

Just as the three-man system reverts to two-man when an umpire goes to the outfield for a call, the four-man will revert to three-man. Once there are runners on base, you will see U2 come inside and you will have four umpires covering each of the four bases so each has all plays and touches at his base.

I mentioned that the importance of outfield coverage should not be underestimated because in the pro game the outfield is huge, the players cover a lot of ground, and there is also the added complication of fans reaching over the fence, like the Jeffrey Maier incident. As a result there are a fair number of plays that revert back to three-man so the next time you are watching a game with four umpires, take note of the number of times you see the plate umpire run up to first or third. With all eyes on the ball, you won't notice the communication going on between umpires but as the ball is in flight, the lead guy, the guy closest to the ball, will be communicating to the trailing umpires which lets them know if they should stay where they are or rotate to another base.

These rotations are not overly complicated on paper but there isn't a lot of time to think on the field. It takes years of experience before they are second nature in real time. This presents a problem in the amateur ranks because three and four-man crews aren't used often, probably only for playoffs and all-star games. Coaches, players and fans will think, "Cool, we've got a full crew" but it isn't necessarily the ideal situation for the umpires themselves. Amidst the pressure of working a game that is more important than most, no matter how much they've studied the mechanics manual, at any moment they may blow a coverage simply because they're a little out of their element.

Almost all amateur four-man crews will make at least one mistake per game but with four umpires, hopefully someone will improvise and cover a call. The players, coaches and fans will hopefully never notice but if there is a close play at a base and there's not an umpire in the neighborhood, it's not going to be pretty. Officiating is not unlike playing a sport; if you're thinking too much out there, you're in trouble. Sometimes less is more, or should I say with four-man mechanics, more is sometimes less.

Balls & Strikes - Timing & Tracking

My premise for "Blues Clues" is that it's a baseball fact-of-life that some calls can go both ways and my objective is to explore the umpiring point-of-view that considers extenuating circumstances in the decision making process, on top of an understanding of basic umpiring mechanics. In "Call 911" I explained that the zone, as written, starts out bigger than you think and that the width of the ball adds another six inches, in-out and hi-low, on top of that. Now I want to look at the physical stuff going on around the plate that dynamically affects how balls and strikes are judged. If I try to mention every single variable I'll be guilty of overkill but, in my effort to educate, I want to focus on the four most important factors that affect the perception of the pitch and the call itself, which often differ: umpire skill, the quality of the pitching, point of view and "framing" by the catcher.

When a batter watches a pitch zip by, it seems like everything stands still, but in reality there are four people, complex humans each, that help shape the scene with their movement. The pitcher may unexpectedly alter his delivery and change his release point, the batter might quietly raise or lower his body based on the height of the pitch, the catcher will shift to stay centered on it and the umpire may blink or take his eyes off the ball, all affecting the outcome. But alas, only one opinion counts, so let's talk about the plate umpire.

The first thing you should notice is that he is positioned behind the catcher but off to the batter's side, the "slot", so he can get the best possible view of the pitch while limiting the chance he is hit with the pitch or a foul tip; he should be squared off facing forward with a wide stance, slightly squat so his chin sits level with the top of the catcher's head. This is sometimes easier said than done when a pitcher has a side-arm delivery and/or a batter hangs over the inside part of the plate; the umpire may have to improvise just so he can see the baseball. Sometimes, he doesn't see the ball until it hits the mitt and in that next second has to make a lot of decisions before making the call; was it a fast ball or a breaking ball, what was the trajectory, did it cut through the zone or bend around it, why did the catcher move his glove afterwards? These are simple questions but when you have to answer four or five of them in a second, it's very easy to think too fast and whatever is blurted out will be the call for the rest of eternity. This is why the single most important factor affecting an umpire's judgment whether at the plate or on the bases, is timing, the slower the better. Some plate umpires will make the call the instant the ball hits the mitt…"pop-strike"…"pop-ball", but the better ones usually go slower…"pop, one thousand and one, strike", "pop, one thousand and two, ball." The difference between a half-second after the ball hits the mitt and two seconds may seem small but in context is huge. Imagine if your income were three or four times what it is now or that you were twice as better looking and charming, if that's possible – haste makes waste even in the smallest of increments!

There is one small casualty of good timing by a plate umpire that you've seen in the classic baseball snippet, "the batter who bolts to first base assuming the pitch he just took is going to be called ball four." This scene plays out like it's from a movie you've watched over and over again on cable TV. No matter how many times you've seen "The Godfather" movies, Fredo ain't coming back from that boat ride and that pitch won't be called a ball either. Everybody thinks the umpire is sticking it to the batter in this situation, he really isn't, but actually is. Let me explain.

Regarding timing, the batter bolting from the box preempts the umpire so his natural response has to be the opposite, a strike call. This is simply a psychological version of Newton's third law, when one body exerts a force on another body, the second body will exert an equal force in the opposite direction. This happens in all kinds of relationships and is not unique to baseball, but let's not go there.

The second thing going on here is that because the batter vacated the premises, before the umpire finished thinking about the pitch, his frame of reference for the strike zone was removed. This is the real issue more so than the Newton thing. The zone is based on the batter and the batter just turned the etch-a-sketch upside down on the umpire; who is going to get the benefit of the doubt now? Beyond calling the pitch himself, and stripping Blue of his reference point, the batter also denied the umpire his normal timing which can't do anything but work against him so seriously, it's not personal, it's just the way nature intended.

While I'm on this topic, I have to tell a related story from a Roy Hobb's League tournament game I played in down in Florida in 2004 that backs up my claim that you have to love baseball because you always see something you've never seen before.

I was playing for a team from Boston, The Braves, and we were going up against a team from Akron in a playoff round. Their clean-up hitter came to the plate in a close game, with a couple of runners on, but first base open. He was a big mean looking dude with a powerful mustache from the 1970's. With a 3-0 count, he took a borderline pitch, dropped his bat and bolted towards first base and as you know, the call could only be a delayed "steeerike!" The guy stopped in his tracks, made a big production out of it and slowly walked back to the plate, taking all day to get back in the box. With a 3-1 count, he took another borderline pitch, dropped the bat and again, bolted for first. "One thousand one, one thousand two, Steeeeerike two!" The guy once again stopped in his tracks, slumped his shoulders making another big production out of it, and began his long dramatic walk back to the box. By this time, our pitcher just couldn't contain himself another second so he jumped into the act, jawing with him on his way back to the plate. Our guy had a hot temper and I remember him mostly for those "Joey Buttafuoco" pants (4) he used to wear well into the new millennium, so let's just say he was no wallflower. Anyway, the trash was flying back and forth and both benches got into it as the scene was set for as exciting a 3-2 pitch as you can imagine in an amateur baseball game. What was our guy gonna do, drill him and put him on or go right after him?

There was no question he was going right after him, it was the only honorable thing to do. After watching five pitches go by without a swing and dragging out the at-bat, drawing the ire of the umpires and the opposing team, the Hulk let loose and I do say "clobbered" one deep to right-center, over the wall that had to have been 400 plus feet, as we were playing in a spacious major league spring training park. If there was ever a guy with a s***-eating grin on his face, it was that SOB who made the slowest trip around the bases you'll ever see. Akron went on to win and this was a great baseball moment. You'll never see that sequence again and it proves a walk is definitely not as good as a hit.

Getting back to the topic at hand, "tracking" refers to the process of watching the pitched ball all the way into the catcher's mitt. You might think this is a no-brainer but let me give you two reasons why it isn't. First, because the umpire is so close to the play, the only way to watch the ball while keeping his head still is to move his eyes rapidly and this is something that isn't natural. You might think this is easy because the umpire sees the ball coming right at him, but the closer it gets to the plate, the sharper the angle is between the umpire's eyes and the ball, especially when it is high, low or wide. Go ahead and try moving your eyes quickly from as far left as they can go to as far right, it can be a little uncomfortable. When you see a pitch from the bench, field or stands, you see the whole scene in the same focal point but when you are just a few feet away, your eyes naturally have to make a rapid adjustment.

If you stop to realize that a pitch moving 70-80-90 miles per hour can move a foot or more in any direction in the last few feet of travel, you can see how important it is to watch the whole pitch. Conversely, when you see the pitch from a distance, you don't have the resolution necessary to distinguish those few inches of movement at the end that shape the call.

The second reason why tracking is more difficult than you imagine comes from the experience of playing baseball. A hitter has to decide if he is going to swing shortly after the pitch is released so he can get the head of the bat out over the plate to drive the ball. Look at any picture of a perfect swing and the bat seems to be making contact with the ball out in front of the stride and the plate, with the batter's eyes looking straight

218

ahead. If the batter decides not to pull the trigger, his head and eyes generally stay in this same position, looking forward. An umpire, who presumably has played a lot of baseball himself, can easily do the same thing. Sure, he is behind the catcher but it's still easy for him to give up on the pitch as it reaches the batter, missing the late action as it crosses the plate. If, however, he has solid tracking, good timing, and a steady head, he will do a better than average job calling balls and strikes.

This idea that the batter stops tracking the ball is something important to think about because we can see, neatly packaged, a common-sense explanation for most disputes between a hitter and umpire; they're not looking at the same thing. The hitter is looking at the pitch from his ideal connect point in the front of the plate (apples). The zone goes all the way to the back point of the plate (oranges). The ball continues its flight until it hits the mitt, which is even deeper still (bananas). When either a player or umpire wonders what the bleep the other guy is looking at, it's a logical question because they clearly aren't seeing the same thing; it's apples and oranges...and bananas.

Point-of-view is everything with balls and strikes; pitchers get ticked off because they only see where the ball is caught and can't sense how a lazy breaking ball curved behind the plate, batters don't see the last three feet of movement and umpires are often fooled by where the ball was caught. If you happen to be another witness either in the field, dugout or stands, you have your own point of view as well. Whether there are fifty people involved in a game or fifty thousand, no two people have the exact same look at the pitch which is the reason why everyone is not on the same page, because they can't be. If it sounds like I am trying to be an apologist for umpires, I apologize. I'm not, I'm just pointing out how anyone can be fooled.

The last item on my list of most important factors affecting ball and strike calls is "framing", the catcher's ability to artfully receive the ball in a way that enhances a pitch's aesthetic qualities, hence the moniker. Framing goes hand in hand with the quality of pitching but before we look at that, let's talk about pitching in general.

Baseball relies on the batters putting the ball in play in order for the game to reach its intended potential. Nobody benefits when there are too many walks so it's incumbent upon the umpire to call strikes to keep the batters swinging so, the poorer the pitching, the more the umpire has to "stretch" the zone, especially when the ball call will yield a walk. Didn't we learn from the Akron story that walks are not exciting? Even when a base on balls forces in the winning run, all you'll hear is the collective sigh of the crowd exhaling in unison the sentiment "what a sucky way to end the game." Okay, that's the last I'll talk about that but what I'm getting at with this "quality" argument is that even when the pitching is outstanding, there are considerations that may cause the umpire to adjust his zone.

Some pitchers have tendencies to pitch in or out, up or down and if he is consistently hitting one spot, the umpire will be more forgiving on that part of the plate and a little less forgiving on the other edges to be fair to the hitters. The more he hits that spot, the more he is rewarded, as opposed to the guy who is all over the place and consistently falls behind. This is not unfair to the hitters because everybody watching knows what's going on so if the batters can't catch on to this pattern, they deserve what they get. It's fair to ask why the same pitch in a vacuum can be viewed differently within the context of the pitcher's particular pattern, but all these factors have real psychological affects on how people see things. I talked earlier about burden of proof and that applies here as well; once the pitcher has established that he doesn't have good control, he bears the burden of re-establishing his ability and credibility with the umpire, by throwing real strikes.

I said quality of pitching goes hand in hand with framing but it's more than that, it's actually a pre-requisite because framing in and of itself shouldn't make a bad pitch look good.

220

The tactic of grabbing a pitch clearly off the plate and pulling the glove back into the strike zone is what I call snatching, which is a pet peeve of mine because if framing is artful, snatching is its grotesque and crude opposite.

This is the same situation as "the batter who bolts to first base" only this time it is the catcher who is preempting the umpire by non-verbally telling everyone that he thinks the pitch was off the plate. "Pop", the ball hits the glove and you can practically hear the catcher's thoughts, "that's a ball but I'll move my glove over here so the umpire will think it's a strike and hopefully he won't see me do this although he is standing a foot away, looking over my shoulder, but what do I have to lose?" I can tell you what he has to lose, a good strike because it's difficult for an umpire to call a snatched pitch a strike because again, the catcher is telling everyone he thought it was wide and if it wasn't wide, he puts the umpire in a position where the strike call makes his judgment questionable. Low grade framing – snatching - is usually only tried by inexperienced catchers. In a way, it's like watching a newborn giraffe fumble around while it finds its legs, but the problem is, it works to a degree in youth baseball so the kids don't realize how silly it looks as they get a little older. I worked a junior varsity game once with a kid who hadn't caught much. After he snatched a wide pitch I told him, "You don't need to do that, just catch it where it's thrown and I'll call it a strike." The next pitch was high about eye level, a ball by any measure, and the kid sticks his arm way up, catches the ball and then holds it there for three seconds. You always have to watch out what you ask for.

Proper framing on the other hand is subtle. It's a combination of how the catcher sets up, uses his body and receives the ball. Rather than snatching side to side, it's more effective if the catcher pulls his mitt back a bit as he receives the ball, subtly sliding his glove a few inches in the direction of the zone so it looks like the movement is simply the extension of the pitch. Since inches matter around the dish, this can make a difference in the umpire's call or at least give him something to work with, going back to the idea of toggling the benefit of the doubt in the moment.

Okay, so we know what framing is and that it can make a pitch look more like a strike than a ball, but you already knew that. I bring it up here to discuss the opposite, when a pitch isn't caught correctly, not snatching, just a ball that is caught awkwardly. There are two schools of thought in umpiring circles. One says "we don't need no stinkin' framing" because a strike is a strike regardless of how it was caught, as long as it goes through the zone. Another says "if it doesn't look like a strike, don't call it a strike."

An umpire has to decide which of these he is going to employ on any given day based on the level and seriousness of play. It is a brave umpire who calls pitches based solely on the actual zone and not to some degree on where they're caught. You might think this is an outrageous statement because the umpire shouldn't care what everybody else thinks but the fan's opinions will always determine what kind of day he has. If he calls a valid strike on a pitch that is caught an inch off the ground, it will look like a bad call to casual observers but if he calls it a ball, nobody will notice. Actually, one guy will notice, the defensive coach; he will not be upset with the umpire, but with his catcher for not catching the ball properly.

In the first case, everybody thinks the umpire screwed up; in the second case one guy quietly thinks his own catcher screwed up. Do you see the difference?

Ironically, when you start umpiring, your intention is to be true to the zone but as you move up, the latter scenario becomes more important, how you look to everyone, not so much for ego's sake but simply for game management. You'll have to shut down complaints from the players and bench and possibly even from the stands as it is not unheard of in amateur baseball to have to give the boot to an out of control booster who won't stop chirping from ten feet away.

Just the other night I saw a perfect example of the perception phenomena in the pros; Texas catcher AJ Pierzynski got thrown out of a game for arguing a ball call with the plate umpire while catching a no-hitter attempt by Yu Darvish. A sharp breaking ball crossed the plate at the knees but was caught well below the strike zone so it was called a ball and Pierzynski snapped. Had the umpire called a strike, it would have looked like he was trying to help out the visiting pitcher in the late innings chasing a no-no. Too often we hear the phrase "perception is reality" which has negative connotations because it implies the truth is compromised. Judging balls and strikes in baseball is a lot more complicated than you realize and to a degree is impacted by perception. While the new Blue-Bots would be very good at ignoring perception, it would also be very difficult to program them for all the other contextual issues that I've discussed, that have a very real and valid place in the game so I think it's a good idea to keep the imperfect human umpires.

In fact, major league umpires do an excellent and consistent job behind the plate and are correct about 95% of the time on average, which is a figure quoted by a pro umpire in a talk he gave to my association. This still leaves ten to fifteen pitches per game that can probably go both ways and keep the game very interesting. So you see, even at the highest level of baseball, those pitches are up for grabs based on the factors I've discussed here as well as some others I haven't considered based only on my amateur experience. You still don't have to agree with any single call but I hope I've demonstrated for you that without the singular motivation of a rooting interest, the impartial umpire has a lot to consider in that split second or two after the ball hits the mitt – "Pop!" – What's it going to be?

The Skinny on Ties

I have to admit that prior to becoming an umpire, I was always impressed by the conviction and accuracy of umpires on close plays at first given what I always saw, a blur, because more often than not, even under the scrutiny of super slow motion, the umps are usually right. My very first week of umpiring high school games found me working a high level varsity contest, however that happened, and the game ended on a 6-4-3 double play where I banged the runner out at first base on a very close play for the final out. All I remember is turning towards first base to discover the same blur I always saw and for some reason I still can't explain, "out" was the call if not the actuality.

Plenty of experienced umpires have schooled me that you simply get good at these over time and the tricks to doing this right have to do with angle, distance, timing and sense of sight and sound, but mostly timing. These calls, and all force plays, are made by watching the runner's foot hit the bag and listening for the sound of the ball hitting the first baseman's glove and figuring out which one is which when it's really close, given that the foot hitting the bag makes a sound too. Just as it is on the dish, timing is the most important thing here because it takes a second or two for the sounds to register, especially when the throw was short hopped to first because you have three sounds to sort out. It's quite possible the first one was the ball hitting the ground, the second is the foot hitting the bag and the third is the ball hitting the glove which can be confusing because normally, if the second sound is the foot, the batter is out but not in this particular case. If you make the call before that sinks in, it's easy to get it wrong.

Another complication is the first baseman's foot coming off the bag which the umpire might not notice if he is too close to the play. It's important you're at a distance that allows you to see the whole picture. I know at times I've tried to be so focused on the foot hitting the base that I didn't notice the fielder had obviously pulled his foot. The saving grace of course, as you should know, is that I had an alert plate umpire watching so we could get the call right. The only other thing you need to know about these calls is that the ideal angle is 90 degrees in relation to the line of the throw so you can see the ball coming across your field of vision which is why the banger on a double play is so tricky. It's hard to get a good angle for the throw to first when it is coming over your shoulder. Yes, that must have been why I blew that call in my first big game; I'm sticking with that. So that's all there really is to these tough calls. Just as my umpiring mentors suggested, they really do get easier with time, but mostly when you find your most comfortable distance and make sure you go slow and watch closely.

Of course, there's no guarantee there will be two different sounds and this is when that old standby comes into play "the tie goes to the runner." There are two ways to investigate this, to look into the rule book and to look at the action on the field. Some people will argue there are no ties and this is true because an umpire cannot call "Tie!" but in terms of sight and sound, ties are as real as Santa Clause, they are and they aren't (Yes, I'm doing my best to twist your melon.) A lot has been written about this so let's look at it with some common sense and start with the rule book.

Rule 6, "The Batter", says the batter is out if **after a third strike or after he hits a fair ball, he or first base is tagged before he touches first base**. So that's it, end of story, the myth is real because if the tag didn't happen first, he is not out, so the tie indeed goes to the runner. Rule 6 is about the batter and this specifically implies when the batter is running to first base.

If this were the only statement in the rule book, there would be no controversy but alas, in the very first sentence of rule 7, "The Runner", the book says **a runner acquires the right to an unoccupied base when he touches it before he is out.** Notice it says "before" so this contradicts the first rule because now, the book is saying if he didn't get there first, he is out, so the tie does not go to the runner after all. The first statement implies a tie goes to the runner and the second statement implies that a tie goes to the defense. This might appear to be a contradiction but it isn't, because rule 6 is specifically about the batter and rule 7 is about the runners. If we look at how the game is played and go back to our friend, the-burden-of-proof, it will make sense that there are two standards.

With regard to the batter, the defense bears the burden to put him out so the ball must arrive first but once he has reached and becomes a runner, the burden to advance is on him so now he must clearly get there first. If you take a minute to step back and think about how baseball is played, this duality fits in perfectly with the spirit of the game. Are you still with me? Let's take a minute to let that sink in because this is a new theory, so relax as you imagine Harry Carey singing "Take Me Out to The Ball Game"…while you enjoy an Old Style at Wrigley:

"Take me out to the ball game,
  Take me out with the crowd;
Buy me some peanuts and Cracker Jack,
  I don't care if I never get back.
Let me root, root, root for the home team,
  If they don't win, it's a shame.
For it's one, two, three strikes, you're out,
  At the old ball gaaaaaame!"

Okay, exhale. So now we know, Alexander Cartright and crew understood there were a couple different dynamics going on out there and the rules must address each, one standard for the batter and one for the runners.

But there is a third reference in the rule book as well, also in rule 7, "The Runner." It says, **he is out if he or the next base is tagged before he touches the next base, after he has been forced to advance by reason of the batter becoming a runner.** What this is telling us is that when a runner is forced, the same standard must apply to him as the one that must apply to the batter. Again, the burden of proof is on the defense.

This makes total sense and solidifies the idea that when the ball is put in play, the burden is on the defense to be first to the punch, but if a runner is advancing on his own, he must win the race. I can't imagine I am the first to piece this together but with so many conflicting opinions out there, it seems to be an important paradigm that has been lost over time. In fact here is statement from, apparently the only umpire who exists, Tim McClelland, when asked about the tie-myth in a Q&A on mlb.com:

> **On-Line Fan**: I am an umpire for Little League. The coach told me that ties go to the runner. I said the batter has to beat the throw to first because there are no such things as ties. Who is right?
> **L.M.F**

> **McClelland**: That is exactly right. There are no ties and there is no rule that says the tie goes to the runner. But the rule book does say that the runner must beat the ball to first base, and so if he doesn't beat the ball, then he is out. So you have to make the decision. That's why umpires are paid the money they are, to make the decision on if he did or if he didn't. The only thing you can do is go by whether or not he beat the ball. If he did, then he is safe.

No sir, the rule doesn't say "the runner must beat the ball to first base", in fact it says the opposite, (the runner is out if) **"first base is tagged before he (the runner) touches first base**." So what we see here is that even at the highest level of umpiring with a seasoned and respected major league guy, there is no distinguishing between batter and runner, hence all the controversy. I said that I would look at it from two perspectives, the rules and the action itself, which is the more practical matter that McClelland is looking at. So perhaps I have found baseball's lost city of Atlantis in the words of the rule book, but I'm not sure how it usually plays out.

Let's start over and again, consider the play when there is only one sound of the ball hitting the glove the moment the runner's foot hits the bag. So what's an umpire to do?

First things first - in a sense, there's no way the umpire can go wrong on these because when the two sounds overlap; it's so close, all everybody sees is a blur and it's pointless for anyone to argue when there is no physical evidence beyond the nanosecond the blur happened. Besides, we know the rules say you can't argue with umpire judgment; half the people will agree with the call.

Close calls, "bangers" in umpiring circles, almost always look safe to everyone in the park based only on the visuals, but if using both sight and sound, like the umpire, it's usually apparent when one sound beats the other. First base coaches who have a lot of experience get pretty good at these too but the ones that don't can cause a lot of problems because they are as close to the play as the umpire, if not too close, and will take their alternative view back to the dugout with them and swear on a stack of bibles that their team was robbed. Very often the only two people at the game who thought the guy was out on the banger will be the two umpires, that is, on top of the defensive team who are happy with the call.

Regarding these plays that are so close they can go either way, there is a practical solution but before I cover that, let me tell you that I've heard umpires discuss this in terms of speed of sound v. speed of light, meaning I suppose, the ball is always a little later than you think because sound is slower than light. If you look at the math however, light travels about a million times faster than sound so...so I'm not even sure what to make of that and besides, I often have trouble counting to three outs, three strikes and four balls. No, the practical matter on perceived ties has to do with the action that preceded it.

Remember when I talked about penalties as opposed to awards? Well this holds true all over the baseball diamond. A batter thinks he was penalized or robbed on a pitch but as we just discussed, the umpire sees the strike call as a reward to the pitcher, especially when he has been hitting his targets all game long. The same is true on the close play at first. If the third baseman made a backhanded stab on a dive and fires a strike across the diamond while on one knee, the umpire is going to reward him for a great play...all day long; this definitely toggles the benefit of the doubt his way.

On the other hand, if it's a routine grounder that the second baseman kicks around a few times before lobbing a throw over that makes it a very close play, well then, he not only kicked the ball but the benefit of the doubt too. I hope this makes sense because if you're a baseball purist you might agree he made an error regardless of the call itself so the burden shifts again and it is his job to clearly beat the runner with the throw.

Fielders can't have it both ways, botch the play and get the benefit of the doubt. The same holds true for runners who lollygag or don't slide, they will lose favor by not playing the game hard or at least well. To me, officiating in a vacuum without considering the essence of the game is a disservice to baseball so how an umpire uses discretion is as important as his ability to judge the play in the first place (5). So you see, ties don't go to the runner or the defense, they go to the umpire.

Redemption

This concludes "Blue Clues." I realize umpire mechanics and points-of-view are an ancillary piece of the baseball puzzle but I feel they complement the larger rules analysis I've presented here. You never have to agree with any call but if you have a better understanding of why some decisions are made, it simply makes you more informed about the game of baseball in the long run.

I look at it like a scene from one of my favorite movies, "The Shawshank Redemption", the story of a man wrongly convicted of murder who never loses hope and after decades of incarceration finally busts free. If you've seen it, you know the last thing Andy Dufresne (Tim Robbins) has to do to win his freedom is crawl through a sewage pipe, "five hundred yards of foulness I can't even imagine" as Morgan Freeman's voiceover declares.

Well, I hope it wasn't quite that bad for you, but I feel the umpire stuff is kind of like that pipe; you need to slog through it to better appreciate the light at the end of the tunnel. If I can get you to shift the image in your mind to the final scene where Andy is on an idyllic beach in Mexico, I want you to consider my alternate but perfect ending to that great film:

```
Red    appears   in   the   background,   a
distant  figure  walking  out  across  the
sand,   wearing   his   cheap   suit   and
carrying his cheap bag.

The  man  on  the  boat  pauses.  Turns
slowly around. Red arrives with a smile
as  wide  as  the  horizon.  The  other  man
raises  his  goggles  and  pulls  down  his
mask. Andy of course.

ANDY: You look like a man who knows how
to get things.

RED: I'm known to locate certain things
from time to time.

Red  shrugs  off  his  jacket,  throws  open
his  beat  up  suit  case  and  pulls  out  two
Mickey  Mantle  model  Rawlings  gloves,  he
dons   the   lefty   version,   tosses   the
other  to  Andy  who  throws  down  his
sander.  With  warm  sunshine  on  their
faces  and  the  Pacific  as  blue  as  it  was
in  Red's  dreams,  Andy  and  Red  have  a
game of catch.

FADE OUT

THE END
```

Part V Footnotes

(1)   Earl Sidney Weaver (1930-2013), Hall of Fame class of 1996 managed for 17 seasons with the Baltimore Orioles from 1968-1982, and 1985-1986. His record was 1480-1060 including a World Series title in 1970. He was ejected from about 100 games, or 1 out of every 15.

(2)   Read it again but this time imagine the voice of Paul Giamatti; that would be awesome. In case you didn't know, Paul is the son of former baseball commissioner Bart Giamatti, whom I quote on the first page of the book.

(3)   I'm talking about the last century and the "OJ" Simpson double-murder trial in case you are too young to remember. Johnnie Cochran was the acclaimed defense attorney who famously made the case, "if it doesn't fit (the glove), you must acquit!" Jackie Chiles is his fictional send-up on the "Seinfeld" series.

(4)   Joseph Buttafuoco (1956) is an auto body shop owner from New York who in his late 30s had an affair with a 16 year old girl, Any Fisher, who shot Buttafuoco's wife in the face, not fatally, in 1992). Buttafuoco became a minor celebrity and the butt of many jokes and parodies, like the "Saturday Night Live" send-up of "Masterpiece Theatre", "House of Buttafuoco". Oh yeah, the pants. His name became synonymous with an early '90s fashion eyesore, these brightly colored and dizzying pants with elastic waist and cuffs, very popular in the young male, Italian-American demographic.

(5)   Instant replay is indeed "the vacuum." How will we feel when an important and amazingly athletic double play turn is reversed because technology proved the shortstop's toe was a hair off the bag? Which call, "safe" or "out" is truer to the game's soul?

A Final Word

Well, that about does her, wraps her all up, although there's a lot more of the story to come, because the game of baseball just keeps giving, perpetuating itself down through the generations, across the sands of time. (Okay, there's your "Big Lebowski" reference).

Just before I finished "The Rules Abide!", I saw something that reminded me why I set out to write it in the first place. I was working a game and a shallow blooper was hit down the right field line that the first baseman chased with his back to the plate, threw his arms up, and completely without intention, deflected the ball about 15 feet to his left where the hustling second baseman completed the catch. I was doing the bases, on the inside, and the runner on second initially tagged up but retreated to second after he saw the second baseman snare it. He looked at me, laughed, and said, "Wow, what a play, I was tagging but had to go back after the deflection." If you know anything about me by now, you know I was thrilled to tell him, "actually, once the first baseman touched it, you could have just kept going...and by the way I have a book coming out that will explain this and a lot of other stuff too..." It was the perfect moment because in an instant, I had one of those you-always-see-something-you've-never-seen-before moments AND a participant who didn't know the rules.

That moment is why I wrote "The Rules Abide!" and why I hope you'll want to tell all your baseball friends all about it. Baseball endures, and the rules abide.

Jim Tosches, September, 2013

For info and bulk book orders, please email:
info@TheRulesAbide.com

Acknowledgements

There aren't words big enough to express my gratitude for all your support and encouragement – Thank You!

Karen Neal
Jim & Kay Schmook
Jane & Corky Gagnon
Joe & Carol Tosches
Frank Rios
Ben Mason
Mark & Karen Ocskasy
Neil McConnell & www.MaxBP.com
Pacific Baseball Umpires Membership
Doug Johnson and NCMSBL Umpire Crew

The Rules Abide!

References

Giamatti Quote	www.goodreads.com
Movie Characters	www.imdb.com
	www.screenplaydb.com
Baseball Participation	www.statista.com
Baseball Rules	official rules, www.mlb.com
Baseball Player info/stats	www.baseball-reference.com
Alexander Cartright	www.wikipedia.com
Kinckerbocker Rules	www.baseballalmanac.com
First Pro Game	www.hobokenbaseball.com
Historical Rules Refs	Jim Evans Pro Baseball School Notes
	Hardball Times
Alvin Dark Quote	www.Snopes.com
Herzog Story	www.reconditebaseball.blogspot.com
BESR/BBCOR	www.baseball.epicsports.com
Modern Baseball News	www.mlb.com
	www.espn.com
Pine Tar Story	McClatchy-Tribune News, 7/24/13
	Wikipedia
Ted Williams Chart	www.TedWilliams.com
Drysdale Streak	www.baseballlibrary.com
Emo Philips Joke	www.theguardian.com 9/28/2005
Connie Mack DH	www.joyofsox.blogspot.com
Fisk-Armbirster	www.youtube.com
	Espn, Wikipedia
3 Men on a base	www.baseball-reference.com
	Wikipedia
Reggie's Hip	www.youtube.com
Eddie Gaedel	Society for American Baseball
	Research (Brian McKenna)
	Wikipedia
	www.baseballalmanac.com
	www.baseball-reference.com
Jeff Maier	Youtube, mlb.com,
	www.nydailynews.com

Made in the USA
San Bernardino, CA
04 October 2013